P9-DDC-686

The Instant Coin Collector

Everything You Need to Know to Get Started **Now**

Arlyn G. Sieber

©2009 Krause Publications

Published by

krause publications
An Imprint of F+W Media, Inc.

700 East State Street • Iola, WI 54990-0001
715-445-2214 • 888-457-2873
www.krausebooks.com

Our toll-free number to place an order or obtain
a free catalog is (800) 258-0929.

All rights reserved. No portion of this publication may be reproduced
or transmitted in any form or by any means, electronic or mechani-
cal, including photocopy, recording, or any information storage and
retrieval system, without permission in writing from the publisher,
except by a reviewer who may quote brief passages in a critical article
or review to be printed in a magazine or newspaper, or electronically
transmitted on radio, television, or the Internet.

Library of Congress Control Number: 2008929067

ISBN-13: 978-0-89689-805-9
ISBN-10: 0-89689-805-9

Designed by Donna Mummery
Edited by Justin Moen

Printed in China

Acknowledgments

The author gratefully acknowledges the following people for their assistance in producing this book:

Brian Allen

Dan Brownell

Kris Kandler

Joe Kertzman

Chet Krause

Justin Moen

Ken Potter

Randy Thern

James Wilcs

Chris Williams

And previous Krause Publications authors whose work provided the basic knowledge for the text that follows.

Contents

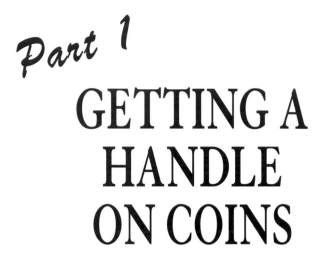

Part 1

GETTING A HANDLE ON COINS

*Basic tips
for
starting out right*

Introduction
Welcome to
Coin Collecting

A gold stater of King Croesus of Lydia.

The kingdom of Lydia, which was located in part of modern-day Turkey, is credited with producing the world's first coins in 700-650 B.C. Some speculate that the world's first coin collector came shortly thereafter.

Coin collecting has provided an enjoyable, educational, and sometimes profitable pastime for generations. The hobby welcomes those of all ages, physical abilities, and financial means. All it requires is an interest in the subject, enjoyment in pursuing a collecting goal, and satisfaction in the completion of that goal. The reward is the pride a collector feels when he or she pulls a coin album off their bookshelf and views a complete collection of a particular coin type or series, or even the progress made toward completing a collection.

Printed references to coin collecting date back as far as the 15th century. In 1796, the hobby generated the first widely circulated book on numismatics: "The Virtuoso's Companion and Coin Collector's Guide," published in England. Coinage was scarce in Colonial America, so there were few coins to collect and even fewer with the financial wherewithal to put coins aside and not spend them.

Congress passed an act establishing the U.S. Mint on April 2, 1792. The decimal coinage system it authorized was based largely on a plan put forth by Thomas Jefferson. The following July, it produced 1,500 silver "half dismes," or five-cent pieces, which are regarded as the nation's first official coinage.

U.S. coinage began in earnest in 1793 with the production of more than 35,000 copper half cents and more than 36,000 copper one-cent coins. By 1796, in addition to half cents and cents, the Mint produced silver half dimes, dimes, quarters,

1792 half disme.

*1793 half-cent (top)
and one-cent coins.*

half dollars, dollars, and gold $2.50, $5, and $10 coins. By the mid-1800s, the Mint was producing about 20 million coins annually in 12 denominations.

The increased production meant more coins to collect, and there were more people who could afford to collect them. A few magazines devoted to coin collecting began to appear in the middle of the century. So did dealers who bought and sold collectible coins for a living or as a supplement to their day jobs. The magazines contained advertisements for collectible coins and oftentimes were produced as house organs and marketing tools by the dealers themselves.

Many collectors of the time also courted relationships with banks, bullion exchange houses, or other volume handlers of coins as sources for their collections. Those who lived near Philadelphia cultivated relationships with officials and employees of the U.S. Mint's production facility located there and, thus, obtained coins directly from the mint.

Interest in coin collecting in the United States surged in the late 1850s when the smaller, copper-nickel Flying Eagle cent replaced the old large copper one-cent coin. Just two years later, the Indian Head cent replaced the Flying Eagle cent. The general public started putting aside the obsolete coins, and demand and prices for them rose. Professional coin dealers emerged to meet the demand, and by the 1870s, most major Eastern cities had coin clubs.

The next major development in coin collecting occurred in 1888 when Dr. George Heath of Monroe, Mich.—a physician by trade who moonlighted as a mail-order coin dealer— published the first issue of *The American Numismatist*. Like many other publications of the time, the magazine was a marketing tool for Heath's coin business. In his new magazine, the country doctor estimated the number of U.S. coin collectors at 20,000.

By 1891, Heath had shortened the serial's title to *The Numismatist*, and its readership formed the basis for the founding of the American Numismatic Association. The ANA continues today as the nation's largest organization for coin collectors, and *The Numismatist* continues as its official monthly journal.

Coin collecting continued to grow in the early 20th century as exciting new designs made old coins obsolete. Ironically, the Great Depression brought another major development in coin collecting that defined the hobby for years to come, and still impacts it today.

In 1934, the Whitman Publishing Co. of Racine, Wis., introduced the "penny board." It was essentially a big piece of cardboard with holes in it for each date and mintmark of Lincoln cents, starting in 1909. The boards sold for 25 cents each and were widely available in hardware stores, dime stores, shoeshine parlors, and gasoline stations.

The large one-cent coin (top) was replaced by a smaller one-cent coin in the late 1850s.

The boards provided cheap entertainment during the economic struggles of the 1930s as

The original Whitman "penny board" was introduced in 1934.

people of all ages checked the one-cent coins in their pocket change for dates and mintmarks that would fill an empty hole in the board. In 1940, the board was reconfigured into a blue folder. The blue Whitman folders, and similar products from other companies, continue today to provide direction in collecting a particular series, and a storage and display medium for collectors.

Coin collecting enjoyed a boom period in the 1950s. War veterans and others had disposable income to devote to a hobby and could find coins of the late 1800s and early 1900s in circulation. What they couldn't find, they could buy from the growing number of dealers who operated shops, set up at coin shows, or advertised in coin publications such as the newly founded *Numismatic News*.

Today, coin collecting is enjoying another renaissance thanks in part to U.S. Mint programs such as the 50 State Quarters and the Westward Journey Nickel Series. Many cities and even smaller towns have coin shops. Major coin auction houses make national headlines when they sell some of numismatics' great rarities. Local, state, and regional organizations for coin collectors meet regularly and sponsor shows where collectors can browse the offerings of dozens or even hundreds of dealers in one spot. Many of these shows also feature non-commercial displays of coins and other numismatic items set up by collectors to the benefit of their fellow hobbyists.

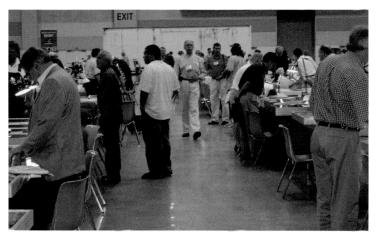

Coin shows big and small bring together collectors and dealers.

The ANA sponsors two shows annually in different cities across the nation. In addition to the bourse floor, the gatherings offer seminars and organization meetings that promote education and camaraderie among fellow collectors. The ANA's headquarters in Colorado Springs, Colo., features a world-class museum open to all and an extensive reference library that members can use for free.

The purpose of this book is to help prospective coin collectors get off to a good start that can lead to a lifetime of enjoyment. Part 1 covers some of the basics one needs to know before popping that first coin in an album.

Part 2 covers 13 series of coins that new collectors can consider for their first pursuit. The emphasis is on coins that can be collected from circulation or purchased at low cost. Some lament that "valuable" coins, such as those collectors were plucking from circulation in the 1950s, can't be found in circulation anymore. But many of the coins that today's veteran hobbyists cut their collecting teeth on weren't "valuable" at the time and have never become valuable. The emphasis wasn't on value; it was on the satisfaction and enjoyment of building a collection. It was on the thrill of finding a long-sought piece needed for a collection.

Having said that, there are still "valuable" coins that can be found in circulation. They may be scarce, but the odds of actually finding one or more increase when collectors know what's valuable and what to look for. Part 3 covers seven series or varieties to watch for when searching circulating coins.

Part 4 provides an illustrated guide to coin terms and an introduction to the all-important topic of grading coins. Part 5 provides tips on taking the next step once a collector feels he or she has mastered the basics. It includes information on the coin community—organizations, publications, and Web sites—and comments and tips on collecting more expensive coins.

The American Numismatic Association's headquarters in Colorado Springs, Colo., includes a world-class museum that is open to the public. Photo courtesy of ANA.

Numismatics (new-miss-MAT-iks)

The study or collection of coins, tokens, and paper money.

U.S. Mint

The official United States Mint (www.usmint.gov) is a branch of the Treasury Department charged with producing the nation's coinage. Its director is appointed by the president.

Private businesses that sometimes concoct official-sounding names that include the words "mint" or "Washington" or other terms sometimes associated with the federal government should not be confused with the official U.S. government mint.

The U.S. Mint's main production facility is located in Philadelphia. Production facilities in Denver, San Francisco, and West Point, N.Y., are known as branch mints.

The U.S. Mint is also in charge of the nation's $100 billion gold and silver reserves. This includes the gold reserves held at the Fort Knox Bullion Depository in Kentucky.

American Numismatic Association

818 North Cascade Ave.
Colorado Springs, CO 80903
(719) 632-2646
www.money.org

Bourse (bors)

The area of a coin show or convention where dealers offer coins for sale. It is often set up in a hotel ballroom or main hall of a convention center.

Chapter 1
How to Handle and Store Coins

So you're about to get a bunch of coins. Now what?

A pile of coins in a coffee can, shoebox, or wrapped up in rolls is just a pile of coins. But organizing them so they can be conveniently stored in some orderly system and viewed on demand makes them a collection. It also preserves them for the long term. They're no longer subject to the wear and tear of circulation.

Many of the suggested series for new collectors covered in Part 2 of this book can be found in circulation or purchased at low cost. Handling and storage considerations for these low-cost coins aren't as critical as they are for, say, a rare silver dollar worth thousands. Still, good habits formed early in a collecting life will pay off later when a collector moves up in rarity and price.

How to handle coins

The less coins are handled, the better. Dirty, oily hands—even if they appear to be clean—lead to dirty, oily coins.

Oftentimes, however, coins have to be handled, particularly when searching circulating coins or when transferring a coin to a holder. When it is necessary to handle a coin, it should be held by the edges between the thumb and forefinger. Avoid contact with the coin's obverse and reverse surfaces.

Also, handle coins over a soft surface so they will not be damaged if accidentally dropped.

Collectible coins should be held between the thumb and forefinger.

Should I clean my coins?

No.

Luster is an important aspect when grading certain high-end coins, but in general, a coin's grade and its corresponding value depend on the amount of wear on the coin, not how shiny it is. Cleaning—particularly home-brewed methods—is often abrasive and will damage a coin rather than improve it.

There may be certain instances when it is desirable to clean a coin, but that is best left to experienced opinions as to when and how.

How to store coins

Folders

Cardboard folders are the most inexpensive and common form of organizing and storing a collection. They can be purchased at many hobby shops and bookstores.

They provide a spot for each date and mintmark in a particular series, thus, acting as a road map for the collector. They are also compact and convenient; they take up little space on a bookshelf and can be pulled down and opened for easy viewing.

Coins collected from circulation can be stored in folders.

The spots for the coins consist of holes in the cardboard sized specially for the particular series covered by the folder. They are meant to be a tight fit so the coins, once inserted, won't fall out. Place the coin in the hole at an angle, so one side of the coin is in the hole. On the side of the coin sticking up, press down and toward the angled side until the coin snaps into place.

The process isn't always graceful; thus, some of the basic rules for handling coins have to be suspended when working with folders. But folders are still suitable for storing coins plucked from circulation and getting started in coin collecting.

2-by-2s

Low- to moderately-priced coins offered for sale at shops and shows are usually stored in cardboard holders commonly called "2-by-2s" because they are two inches square. They consist of two pieces with a clear Mylar window in the center. The coin is placed between the two pieces, which are then stapled together.

These 2-by-2 holders are also inexpensive. They are suitable for long-term storage and offer a number of advantages over the basic folder:

— The window in the holder allows both sides of the coin to be viewed.

— The entire coin is enclosed.

— The coin can be handled by the edges when inserted into the holder.

Dealers often sell coins in 2-by-2 holders, which can be stored in specially designed boxes.

As for disadvantages:

– Storing an entire collection of a particular series takes up more space.

– The coins can be viewed only one at a time.

– Caution should be used when inserting or removing coins from the holders to make sure the staples' sharp edges don't damage the coins.

– There is no road map to the series. A separate checklist is needed.

The 2-by-2 holders can be stored in long, narrow boxes specially sized to hold them. They can also be inserted into pockets in a plastic page, which can then be inserted into a three-ring binder.

Originally, the plastic pages contained polyvinylchloride, which produced a soft, flexible pocket. But the substance breaks down over time, resulting in a green slime that could contact the coins. Manufacturers then started substituting Mylar for the PVC. The Mylar does not break down, but the page containing it is more brittle and not as flexible.

Flips

Similar in size to the cardboard 2-by-2s, plastic "flips," to use the common vernacular, are another common storage method for coins for sale. They consist of a plastic pocket, into which the coin is inserted, with a flap that folds down over the pocket. Coin dealers will often staple the flap shut.

Flips offer many of the same advantages as the cardboard 2-by-2s:

– Although they cost more, flips are still inexpensive.

– The entire coin is enclosed.

– Both sides of the coin can be viewed.

– The coin can be handled by the edges when being inserted into the holder.

Also, they don't have to be stapled shut, thus, eliminating the possibility of the staples scratching the coin.

The big disadvantage to flips is their composition. They, too, originally contained polyvinylchloride. Manufacturers then started making flips containing Mylar, but the resulting product again is more brittle and not as flexible as the old PVC flips.

Plastic "flips" are another common storage method for coins sold at shows and shops.

For long-term storage, it's best to remove coins from flips and transfer them to another type of holder.

Albums

Coin albums are a step up from the basic folder. They are in book form and contain a hole for each date and mintmark in the particular series covered. The hole has a clear plastic back and a clear plastic front. The plastic front slides out, and the coin can be placed in the hole. The plastic front is then slid back over the hole.

Albums combine many of the advantages of 2-by-2s and folders:

– They are compact and convenient, and can be stored on a bookshelf.

– They are affordable.

– Both sides of the coin can be viewed.

Coin albums protect both sides of a coin but also allow both sides to be viewed.

- Their labeled holes act as a road map to a series.
- The entire coin is enclosed.
- The coin can be handled by the edges when being inserted.

The disadvantage to albums is that sliding the plastic front can damage a coin in the holder if the plastic rubs against the coin. Thus, albums are not recommended for expensive uncirculated coins.

Hard-plastic holders

Hard-plastic holders are the top of the line in coin storage, but are still affordable. They consist of two pieces with one or more clear windows through which the coin can be viewed. The two pieces are held together with plastic screws or snapped together.

To insert a coin into the holder, the two pieces are separated and the coin is placed face up into the bottom piece.

The top piece is then placed over the bottom piece, and the two pieces are screwed or snapped together again.

Some of the world's great numismatic rarities are stored in hard-plastic holders. They offer all of the advantages of the less expensive storage methods but in a safe, inert environment.

Slabs

In 1986, a group of coin dealers formed the Professional Coin Grading Service. For a fee, dealers and collectors could submit coins to the service and receive a professional opinion on their

Hard plastic holders are the top of the line in coin storage.

The Professional Coin Grading Service was the first grading service to encapsulate coins after grading.

Other grading services followed PCGS' lead in encapsulating coins after grading.

grades. After grading, a coin is encapsulated in an inert hard-plastic holder with a serial number and the service's opinion on its grade indicated on the holder.

The concept was successful, and several competing services were established in succeeding years. Today, most coins valuable enough to justify the grading fee have been graded by one of the services and encapsulated in its holder.

The grading-service holders are common at coin shows and shops, and acquired the nickname "slabs." The holders are suitable for long-term storage of high-end collectible coins.

Obverse

The face or "heads" side of a coin.

Reverse

The back or "tails" side of a coin.

Mintmark

A small letter or other mark on a coin indicating where it was minted. Current U.S. coinage carries either a "D" mintmark for Denver, "P" for Philadelphia, "S" for San Francisco, or "W" for West Point, N.Y. Most U.S. coins without mintmarks were minted in Philadelphia.

Mylar

A DuPont trademark for a strong polyester film.

Part 2

HOW TO
GET STARTED

*Coin series and
strategies
for new collectors*

1964-P   BU-MS-63

7.50

Chapter 2
Collecting
Lincoln Memorial Cents

*1982-S proof Lincoln
Memorial cent.*

Ask a longtime coin collector about the first series he or she collected, and they will probably say Lincoln cents. U.S. one-cent coins have been a staple for new collectors since the Whitman Publishing Co. introduced its venerable "penny board" in the 1930s. This tradition continued as the board evolved into a folder in the 1940s.

The U.S. Mint now produces billions of one-cent coins a year, so there is little to no chance that any one of them popped into a folder today will command a substantial numismatic premium in the future. But the basic premise of collecting one-cent coins—the satisfaction of pursuing and ultimately completing a series collection—has not changed since the penny board was introduced in 1934.

The collecting knowledge gained by pursuing one-cent coins can provide the foundation for a positive experience when moving up the collecting value ladder. Any mistakes made at this level are a cheap education that can pay off big in the future.

The story behind the coin

The Lincoln cent was introduced in 1909 to commemorate the centennial of Abraham Lincoln's birth.

Lincoln thus became the first president to be depicted on circulating U.S. coinage.

Designer Victor David Brenner fashioned the bust of Lincoln on the obverse. His design for the reverse consisted of the words "One Cent" framed by two wheatears. Lincoln cents with this reverse design are commonly referred to as "wheat cents."

The reverse design was changed in 1959 to commemorate the 150th anniversary of Lincoln's birth. Designer Frank Gasparro composed a depiction of the Lincoln Memorial in Washington, D.C., which replaced the wheatears design on the reverse.

The Lincoln cent originally featured a wheatears design on its reverse.

Where to get them

Sources for a Lincoln Memorial cent collection are as close as one's pocket. Collectors can check their pocket change for dates and mintmarks that fill empty spots in their collection.

Pocket change is a particularly good source for current-year or recent-year issues. Clean, brightly-colored specimens with little wear can be found and put aside for a collection. When a new year begins, start watching pocket change for coins with the new dates. Even older Lincoln Memorial cents, dating back to the 1960s or even 1959, can be found in pocket change.

To fill a collection more quickly, search a larger quantity of coins, such as change from a small business, if possible. Or, obtain several rolls of one-cent coins from your bank.

A search of five rolls of one-cent coins (top) filled 64 of the 90 holes in a Lincoln Memorial cent album.

In an exercise for this book, five rolls of one-cent coins (250 coins total) were obtained from a local bank. Also gathered for the exercise was a Whitman folder for Lincoln Memorial cents from 1959 through 1998, a 5X magnifying glass, a container in which the unneeded coins could be placed, and a soft surface on which to work.

The search of the five rolls produced 64 of the 90 coins needed to fill the folder. Predictably, most of the missing coins were the earlier issues from the 1960s. But the oldest coins found were a 1959-D, 1960-D, and a 1961.

The search took a couple of hours, which can help pass the time on a rainy or snowy weekend afternoon. It can also bring together a parent and child when the search is a joint project between the two.

Mintmarks

Lincoln Memorial cents have either no mintmark, a "D" indicating the coin was struck at the Denver Mint, or, starting in 2001, a "P" for the Philadelphia Mint. Those without mintmarks were struck at either Philadelphia (1959-2000) or West Point (1973-1986).

The San Francisco Mint ("S" mintmark) produced cents for circulation from 1968 through 1974. Starting in 1975, it produced S-mintmark cents for inclusion only in special collector sets (proof and mint sets).

The mintmark appears below the date on the obverse of Lincoln Memorial cents. A magnifying glass helps decipher them.

Condition

As the rolls were searched in the exercise noted above, coins that filled a hole in the folder were temporarily placed over the hole rather than immediately inserted into it. When a duplicate of a date and mintmark was found, it was compared to the previous example, and the coin in better condition was kept.

When comparing Lincoln cents, it is tempting to automatically keep the shiniest example of a particular date and mintmark. Original, bright-bronze color on a cent does indeed indicate a coin that has seen little circulation.

But also check for wear on the design's high points. On a cent, these include Lincoln's cheekbone and the detail in his hair. A magnifying glass and incandescent lighting aid in examining a coin's condition.

How to store them

As indicated earlier, an inexpensive folder is just fine for storing Lincoln Memorial cents plucked from circulation. The 2-by-2 holders could also be used if desired. Or, a collector could keep a few 2-by-2 holders handy in case he or she comes across a coin that, for whatever reason, they deem worthy of a little extra protection.

Lincoln's cheekbone and hair are key points to check for wear when grading Lincoln cents.

Lincoln Memorial cent specs

Obverse designer: Victor David Brenner.

Reverse designer: Frank Gasparro.

Diameter: 19 millimeters.

Composition (1959-1982): copper-zinc.

Weight (1959-1982): 3.11 grams.

Composition (1982-date): copper-plated zinc.

Weight (1982-date): 2.5 grams.

Cent quiz

Question: How many pennies does the U.S. Mint produce in a year? Answer: None.

Officially, the Mint does not strike "pennies;" it strikes "one-cent coins." A penny is a traditional British denomination.

Although knowledgeable and longtime collectors may still informally call U.S. one-cent coins "pennies," the majority refer to them more accurately as "cents."

Lincoln Memorial cent checklist

_____ 1959
_____ 1959-D
_____ 1960
_____ 1960-D
_____ 1961
_____ 1961-D
_____ 1962
_____ 1962-D
_____ 1963
_____ 1963-D
_____ 1964
_____ 1964-D
_____ 1965
_____ 1966
_____ 1967
_____ 1968
_____ 1968-D
_____ 1968-S

1964-D Lincoln Memorial cent. Note the mintmark location below the date on the obverse.

_____ 1969	_____ 1980
_____ 1969-D	_____ 1980-D
_____ 1969-S	_____ 1981
_____ 1970	_____ 1981-D
_____ 1970-D	_____ 1982
_____ 1970-S	_____ 1982-D
_____ 1971	_____ 1983
_____ 1971-D	_____ 1983-D
_____ 1971-S	_____ 1984
_____ 1972	_____ 1984-D
_____ 1972-D	_____ 1985
_____ 1972-S	_____ 1985-D
_____ 1973	_____ 1986
_____ 1973-D	_____ 1986-D
_____ 1973-S	_____ 1987
_____ 1974	_____ 1987-D
_____ 1974-D	_____ 1988
_____ 1974-S	_____ 1988-D
_____ 1975	_____ 1989
_____ 1975-D	_____ 1989-D
_____ 1976	_____ 1990
_____ 1976-D	_____ 1990-D
_____ 1977	_____ 1991
_____ 1977-D	_____ 1991-D
_____ 1978	_____ 1992
_____ 1978-D	_____ 1992-D
_____ 1979	_____ 1993
_____ 1979-D	_____ 1993-D

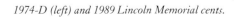

1974-D (left) and 1989 Lincoln Memorial cents.

_____	1994	_____	2002-P
_____	1994-D	_____	2002-D
_____	1995	_____	2003 P
_____	1995-D	_____	2003-D
_____	1996	_____	2004-P
_____	1996-D	_____	2004-D
_____	1997	_____	2005-P
_____	1997-D	_____	2005-D
_____	1998	_____	2006-P
_____	1998-D	_____	2006-D
_____	1999	_____	2007-P
_____	1999-D	_____	2007-D
_____	2000	_____	2008-P
_____	2000-D	_____	2008-D
_____	2001-P		Series is ongoing.
_____	2001-D		

The new Lincoln cents

The Lincoln cent reverse was scheduled to change again in 2009 to commemorate the bicentennial of Lincoln's birth. A law passed Sept. 27, 2006, requires the U.S. Mint to strike 2009-dated circulating Lincoln cents with four different reverse designs emblematic of various stages of Lincoln's life: (1) his birth and early childhood in Kentucky, (2) his formative years in Indiana, (3) his professional life in Illinois, and (4) his presidency.

The law further mandates that after 2009 the Lincoln cent reverse design will represent Lincoln's "preservation of the United States of America as a single and united country."

The law also mandates that Victor David Brenner's obverse design continue to be used.

Change in the change

In 1982, the cent's composition changed from predominately copper alloyed with zinc to predominately zinc plated with copper. Coins in both compositions were struck in that year.

They can be distinguished by weight. The predominately copper composition weighs 3.11 grams; the predominately zinc composition weighs 2.5 grams.

Some folders contain holes for both compositions. Collectors without the means to weigh the coins should not fret this distinction in compiling their collections. There is no difference in numismatic value between the two compositions.

Cent production

In 2007, the Philadelphia Mint struck more than 3.7 billion one-cent coins, and the Denver Mint struck more than 3.6 billion one-cent coins. Total 2007 circulating cent production was more than 7.4 billion. The 1968-S has the lowest mintage among Lincoln Memorial cents struck for circulation: 261,311,510.

Get in the loupe

A magnifying glass is an essential tool of coin collecting. It allows a collector to view details on a coin, especially when examining a coin's condition.

A magnifying glass of about 5X is fine for most beginning to intermediate coin-collecting pursuits and is affordable.

A 5X magnifying glass.

Small vs. large

There are three years of circulating Lincoln Memorial cents—1960, 1970 and 1982 — with slight design variations in the dates. These are commonly referred to as "small date" and "large date" because of the difference in size between the two variations.

1960 small date. *1960 large date.*

The 1960 small date struck at Philadelphia is worth about $2 retail in higher circulated grades, but the rest do not vary substantially above face value in circulated grades.

1970 small date. *1970 large date.*

Some folders or albums may contain holes for the date variations.

1982 small date. *1982 large date.*

Cent quiz

Question: How many images of Lincoln appear on the Lincoln Memorial cent? Answer: Two.

The first, of course, is the bust of Lincoln on the obverse. For the second, look closely in the middle of the Lincoln Memorial on the reverse on a new or newer cent. An outline of the Lincoln statue that appears in the real Lincoln Memorial can be seen on the coin.

Chapter 3
Collecting the
Westward Journey Nickel Series

The year 2004 saw the first significant change in the design of the Jefferson five-cent coin since its introduction in 1938. The result is a short series with pleasing designs that is within the reach of any collector. It's an excellent series for new collectors.

"Ocean in view!" reverse in the Westward Journey Nickel Series.

The story behind the coin

Felix Schlag's renditions of Thomas Jefferson and his Virginia home, Monticello, made their debut on the five-cent coin in 1938. They replaced the Buffalo nickel, which remains popular with collectors today.

The Jefferson nickel saw some changes during the war years of 1942-1945. The composition was changed from copper-nickel to copper, silver, and manganese. To mark the change, the mintmark was moved from below the date on the obverse to above the dome on Monticello on the reverse.

The Jefferson nickel (top) replaced the Buffalo nickel in 1938.

In 1946, the Jefferson nickel reverted to its original composition and design. They remained unchanged until 2004, when Congress authorized new designs to commemorate the bicentennial of Lewis

The Jefferson nickel's composition changed during the war years of 1942-1945.

and Clark's exploration of the Louisiana Territory. As president, Jefferson authorized the mission to find the "most direct & practicable water communication across this continent for the purpose of commerce."

The story behind the designs

For 2004, the obverse retained Schlag's bust of Jefferson, which was originally based on a bust by sculptor Jean-Antoine Houdon. The two reverses for 2004 are known as the peace medal design and the keelboat design.

The peace medal reverse (top) in the Westward Journey Nickel Series is based on the design of Indian peace medals carried by Lewis and Clark.

The peace medal design is based on the original design for an Indian peace medal commissioned for Lewis and Clark's expedition. It features two clasped hands. The wrist of one hand is adorned with the cuff of a military uniform; the wrist of the other hand is adorned with beads and a stylized American eagle.

The design was meant to symbolize friendship between the American government and the Native Americans that Lewis and Clark would encounter on their exploration. Lewis and Clark carried the medals with them and gave them to Native American leaders as a goodwill gesture.

2004 Jefferson nickel with the keelboat reverse design.

The keelboat design depicts the type of watercraft Lewis and Clark used in their expedition. The two uniformed figures in the boat's bow represent the two explorers.

For 2005, the traditional bust of Jefferson on the obverse was replaced by another design also based on a Houdon

The traditional bust of Jefferson was changed on 2005 nickels. The bison reverse is shown at left.

sculpture. But instead of the traditional full view, the coin focuses on Jefferson's face from the front hairline of his right temple forward. The word "Liberty" in script on the obverse is based on Jefferson's own handwriting.

Two different reverse designs were also used in 2005— the American bison design and the "Ocean in view!" design.

The American bison design is reminiscent of the so-called Buffalo nickel, which was struck from 1913 until the Jefferson nickel replaced it in 1938. Lewis and Clark's journals described the animal, which was important to the Native American culture.

The "Ocean in view!" reverse design was inspired by a Nov. 7, 1805, entry in William Clark's journal: "We are in view of the opening of the Ocean, which Creates great joy." The view of the Pacific Ocean in the design is based on a photograph by Andrew E. Cier of Astoria, Ore.

For 2006, the obverse design changed again. The new image was based on a Rembrandt Peale portrait of Jefferson in 1800, when Jefferson was 57 years old and just before he became president. The word "Liberty" is again in

Yet another depiction of Jefferson was used on 2006 nickels, while the reverse reverted to the traditional depiction of Monticello.

script based on Jefferson's handwriting.

The 2006 reverse returned to the traditional view of Monticello as it originally appeared on the Jefferson nickel. But contemporary Mint engravers enhanced Schlag's original work, restoring more detail and relief to the design.

The result, according to the Mint, is a "crisper and more detailed" image.

Mintmarks

Westward Journey five-cent coins struck for circulation have either a "P" mintmark for Philadelphia or a "D" mintmark for Denver. The mintmark appears on the obverse on all of the coins in the series. It is below the date on the 2004 and 2006 issues. It is below the word "Liberty" on the 2005 issues.

Where to get them

Nice examples of the Westward Journey Nickel Series are easily found in circulation. A watchful eye on pocket change over time should complete a series collection.

Searching large quantities of change will again speed up the process. A search of five rolls of nickels (200 coins) obtained from a local bank produced six of the 10 reverse design, date, and mintmark combinations required to complete the series:

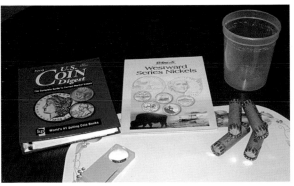

Searching rolls of nickels is a good way to find coins in the Westward Journey Series.

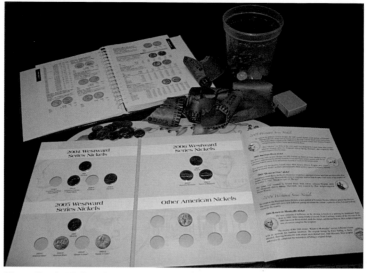

Five rolls of nickels yielded six of the 10 reverse design, date, and mintmark combinations in the Westward Journey Series.

(1) 2004-D peace medal.

(2) 2004-D keelboat.

(3) 2005-D bison.

(4) 2005-D "Ocean in view!"

(5) 2006-P Monticello.

(6) 2006-D Monticello.

It also produced duplicates for each date, which filled the holes for display of the obverse design alongside the reverse designs for each year.

That left just four coins to complete the series:

(1) 2004-P peace medal.

(2) 2004-P keelboat.

(3) 2005-P bison.

(4) 2005-P "Ocean in view!"

The lack of Philadelphia-produced coins in the sample rolls probably reflects the region in which they were obtained. Still, a close watch on pocket change or searching additional rolls should eventually complete the collection.

Check all the dates

The distinctive obverse and reverse designs made the Westward Journey five-cent coins stand out when the rolls were opened and dumped onto a soft surface for examination. But the date on each coin in the rolls was still checked and produced some additional keepers.

They were: one 1939, one 1940, one 1946-D, two 1961-D coins, one 1963-D, nine 1964 coins (seven with "D" mintmarks and two with no mintmarks, indicating they were struck at Philadelphia), and one 1966. One of the 1964-D coins was in such good condition that it could easily have been mistaken for a more recent issue at first glance.

Putting aside these coins can form the basis for taking the Jefferson series back to its debut in 1938. Because five-cent coins do not contain precious metals, they have not been cherry picked over the years as much as the higher denominations, which contained silver until 1965. There are still realistic chances of finding older issues, such as those cited above, in circulation.

Condition

As with the search for Lincoln Memorial cents in Chapter 2, duplicates were compared and the better example was kept. As needed examples were found, they were laid over

The five rolls of nickels also yielded coins dated 1939 (from top), 1940, and 1946.

the holes and not inserted into the albums until the search was complete.

On the traditional bust of Jefferson on the obverse, the cheekbone is one of the high points to check for wear. On all examples, also check for detail in the hair and nice, clean surfaces with a minimum of scratches.

On the traditional reverse depiction of Monticello, the steps have long been a focal point. Look for sharp, clearly defined steps leading up to the building's entrance.

How to store them

Folders provide suitable, handy, and attractive storage for Westward Journey five-cent pieces obtained in circulation. The 2-by-2 holders are also practical alternatives if desired.

Jefferson nickel specs

Obverse designer (2004): Felix Schlag.

Obverse designers (2005): Joe Fitzgerald and Don Everhart II.

Obverse designers (2006): Jamie N. Franki and Donna Weaver.

Reverse designer (2004 peace medal): Norman E. Nemeth.

Father of the nation's coinage

Today's decimal monetary system in the United States is based largely on a proposal put forth by Thomas Jefferson in the country's early days. His original coinage plan called for the dollar as the basic monetary unit and included several minor coins and a gold $10.

Reverse designer (2004 keelboat): Al Maletsky.

Reverse designers (2005 bison): Jamie Franki and Norman E. Nemeth.

Reverse designers (2005 "Ocean in view!"): Joe Fitzgerald and Donna Weaver.

Reverse designers (2006 Monticello): Felix Schlag and John Mercanti.

Diameter: 21.2 millimeters.

Composition: copper-nickel.

Weight: five grams.

Westward Journey Nickel Series checklist

_____ 2004-P peace medal.

_____ 2004-D peace medal.

_____ 2004-P keelboat.

_____ 2004-D keelboat.

_____ 2005-P bison.

_____ 2005-D bison.

_____ 2005-P "Ocean in view!"

_____ 2005-D "Ocean in view!"

_____ 2006-P Monticello.

_____ 2006-D Monticello.

Where's the "S"?

The San Francisco Mint no longer strikes coins for circulation, but it still produces specially prepared coins for inclusion in collector sets, such as proof sets. These coins have an "S" mintmark.

Still the same

Except for the war years of 1942-1945, the U.S. nickel five-cent coin has been struck in the same size (21.2 millimeters), weight (five grams), and composition (copper-nickel) since the Liberty nickel was introduced in 1883.

Know your values

Whenever searching bulk quantities of coins, have a value guide, such as the book "U.S. Coin Digest" or the magazine *Coin Prices*, available for reference. These references list the approximate retail values for coins.

Any older dates found should be checked in the guide to see if their values are above the norm. If they are, proper handling and storage methods should be followed to preserve the coins.

1896 Liberty nickel.

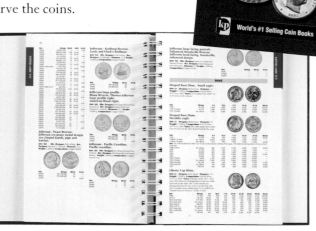

The book "U.S. Coin Digest" has a complete listing of U.S. coins and their values in various grades.

Chapter 4
Collecting the Bicentennial Coins

There once was a time when a Bicentennial quarter was a common part of one's pocket change. But now, more than 30 years after their release, Bicentennial coins, particularly the quarters, have become scarcer in circulating change.

With a little bit of effort, however, a nice set of Bicentennial coins can be put together for little cost. The resulting set provides a pleasing keepsake of our nation's 200th birthday.

Bicentennial quarter.

The story behind the coins

A variety of coinage proposals for the nation's Bicentennial emerged in the years leading up to the celebration. Among them were proposals for special commemorative coins (the U.S. Mint had not issued commemorative coins since 1954), redesigning all six circulating coins, issuing a two-cent coin with a Bicentennial design, and issuing a gold commemorative coin.

The Mint and Treasury Department initially resisted any changes to circulating coin designs and the issuance of commemorative coins, but they eased their opposition as the various proposals were winnowed to a final bill that

Bicentennial half dollar.

was signed into law Oct. 18, 1973, by President Richard M. Nixon. That bill called for quarters, half dollars, and dollar coins struck after July 4, 1975, to bear new reverse designs emblematic of the nation's Bicentennial. The law also called for the coins to bear the dual date "1776-1976."

The law further authorized the Mint to strike the Bicentennial coins in a 40-percent silver composition (rather than the copper-nickel clad composition of the circulation strikes) for inclusion in three-coin mint and proof sets for sale directly to collectors. The San Francisco Mint struck these special coins, which bear an "S" mintmark.

Bicentennial dollar.

The San Francisco Mint also produced proof versions of all three coins in the circulating clad composition for inclusion in regular annual proof sets.

To select designs for the Bicentennial coins, the Mint sponsored a contest open to all U.S. citizens. The winners were announced in March 1974:

- A Revolutionary-era drummer-boy design, submitted by Jack L. Ahr of Arlington Heights, Ill., was selected for the quarter.
- A depiction of Independence Hall, submitted by Seth G. Huntington of Minneapolis, was selected for the half dollar.

– A depiction of the Liberty Bell superimposed over the moon, submitted by Dennis R. Williams of Columbus, Ohio, was selected for the dollar. The moon was symbolic of the nation's lunar landings and exploration.

The Bicentennial coinage law gave the Treasury secretary the authority to determine how long the special reverse designs would be used. In September 1976, the Mint announced that Treasury Secretary William E. Simon had ordered the Mint to revert back to the old reverse designs with the beginning of 1977-dated coinage.

Where to get them

Bicentennial quarters still turn up occasionally in circulation, but not as often as they once did. A careful watch on pocket change should eventually produce an example.

Rolls from banks are potential sources for Bicentennial coins.

Five rolls of quarters from a local bank yielded the Bicentennial coin shown above and coins dated 1965 and 1966.

Five rolls of quarters acquired from a local bank (200 coins total) turned up just one example, with a "D" mintmark. The same rolls produced two 1965-dated quarters and two 1966-dated quarters. The presence of the older coins in higher numbers may indicate that more people are putting aside the Bicentennial quarters as they encounter them in circulation. Also, more people are paying closer attention to the quarters in their pocket change thanks to the 50 State Quarters Program.

Rolls may be the best bet for acquiring Bicentennial half dollars from circulation.

Although the Mint still strikes half dollars for circulation, few of the big, bulky coins are actually used. Thus, rolls may be the best bet for acquiring Bicentennial half dollars from circulation. A five-roll sample (100 coins total) from a local bank yielded 10 Bicentennial half dollars, all with a "D" mintmark.

Even bigger and bulkier are the Eisenhower dollars with the Bicentennial reverse designs. The Eisenhower dollar was struck from 1971 to 1978; it was replaced by the smaller Anthony dollar in 1979.

That makes the Eisenhower dollar an obsolete design in a coin denomination that has never been popular among the public. A collector may be able to find a bank here and there that still has some.

Bicentennial dollar coins can be acquired at coin shows and shops.

A better bet, however, is a local coin shop or show. Nice examples in uncirculated grades should be available at either for just a few dollars each. They also give new collectors a low-cost introduction to buying coins over the counter.

Shows and shops are also good sources for Bicentennial half dollars (top) and quarters in uncirculated grades.

On Bicentennial quarters, the mintmark is located on the obverse just behind the bow in Washington's hair.

Local shops and shows are also good sources for nice examples of the Bicentennial quarters and half dollars. Examples plucked from circulation will be well worn; a little extra money spent on purchased examples will produce a much nicer set.

Expect to find the 40-percent-silver proof and mint sets at shops and shows, too. According to the book "U.S. Coin Digest," the Bicentennial three-coin mint set sells for about $15, and the Bicentennial three-coin proof set sells for about $20.

Mintmarks

All three denominations of Bicentennial coins have either no mintmark, indicating they were struck at Philadelphia, or a "D" mintmark for Denver. Special collector versions struck for mint and proof sets, including the 40-percent-silver versions, have an "S" mintmark for San Francisco.

On the quarter, the mintmark is on the obverse just behind the bow in Washington's hair on the lower right. On the half dollar, the mintmark is on the obverse just below Kennedy's neck. On the dollar, the mintmark is on the obverse just below Eisenhower's neck.

Condition

On the quarter, Washington's cheek and the hair around his ear are key points to check for wear. On the half dollar, the cheek and hair are again key points. In particular, check for detail in the hair between the part in Kennedy's hair and his ear. On the dollar, Eisenhower's cheek and jawbone are also key points.

How to store them

Folders are fine for Bicentennial coins plucked from circulation, but better examples purchased at shops and shows deserve a step up in storage systems. Nice examples of Bicentennial coins purchased individually at shows or shops will probably come in 2-by-2 holders. These are fine for long-term storage of these coins. So are hard-plastic holders, which can house coins either individually or as a set.

If you take purchased coins out of their 2-by-2 holders to transfer them to another storage system, observe all the rules for safe handling of coins:

- Handle them by the edges between your thumb and forefinger.
- Don't touch the obverse or reverse surfaces.
- Work over a soft surface.
- Be careful when removing coins from a 2-by-2 so the staples don't scratch the coin.
- Be equally careful when placing the coin into its new holder.

Bicentennial coin specs

Quarter (circulation strikes and proof sets):

Obverse designer: John Flanagan.

Reverse designer: Jack L. Ahr.

Diameter: 24.3 millimeters.

Weight: 5.67 grams.

Composition: Clad layers of 75-percent copper and 25-percent nickel bonded to a pure-copper core.

Quarter (silver mint and proof sets):

Weight: 5.75 grams.

Composition: Clad layers of 80-percent silver and 20-percent copper bonded to a core of 20.9-percent silver and 79.1-percent copper.

Total silver weight: 0.0739 troy ounces.

Half dollar (circulation strikes and proof sets):

Obverse designer: Gilroy Roberts.

Reverse designer: Seth Huntington.

Diameter: 30.6 millimeters.

Weight: 12.5 grams.

Composition: Clad layers of 75-percent copper and 25-percent nickel bonded to a pure-copper core.

Half dollar (silver mint and proof sets):
Weight: 11.5 grams.
Composition: 40-percent silver, 60-percent copper.
Total silver weight: 0.148 troy ounces.

Dollar (circulation strikes and proof sets):
Obverse designer: Frank Gasparro.
Reverse designer: Dennis R. Williams.
Diameter: 38.1 millimeters.
Weight: 22.68 grams.
Composition: 75-percent copper and 25-percent nickel bonded to a pure-copper core.

Dollar (silver mint and proof sets):
Weight: 24.59 grams.
Composition: Clad layers of 80 percent silver and 20-percent copper bonded to a core of 20.9-percent silver and 79.1-percent copper.
Total silver weight: 0.3161 troy ounces.

Bicentennial coinage checklist
Circulation strikes:
_____ 1976 quarter
_____ 1976-D quarter
_____ 1976 half dollar
_____ 1976-D half dollar
_____ 1976 dollar
_____ 1976-D dollar

Silver mint and proof sets:
_____ 1976-S uncirculated quarter
_____ 1976-S proof quarter
_____ 1976-S uncirculated half dollar
_____ 1976-S proof half dollar
_____ 1976-S uncirculated dollar
_____ 1976-S proof dollar

Bicentennial coinage mintages
Circulation strikes

Date, mintmark	Denomination	Mintage
1976	Quarter	809,784,016
1976-D	Quarter	860,118,839
1976	Half dollar	234,308,000
1976-D	Half dollar	287,565,248
1976	Dollar	117,337,000
1976-D	Dollar	103,228,274

Proofs, clad composition

1976-S	Quarter	4,149,730
1976-S	Half dollar	7,059,099
1976-S	Dollar	7,059,099

Mint sets, silver composition

1976-S	Quarter	4,908,319
1976-S	Half dollar	4,908,319
1976-S	Dollar	4,908,319

Proof sets, silver composition

1976-S	Quarter	3,998,621
1976-S	Half dollar	3,998,621
1976-S	Dollar	3,998,621

Two cents' worth

The proposal to strike a two-cent coin for the nation's Bicentennial had precedent. The U.S. Mint issued circulating two-cent coins in a copper-tin-zinc composition from 1864 through 1872. It also struck about 1,100 proof two-cent pieces in 1873.

Type I and type II dollars

Two styles of lettering appear on the reverse of the Eisenhower Bicentennial dollar coins with the clad composition—both circulation strikes and proofs. Bicentennial dollars struck in 1976 use thinner letters in "United States of America" and "One Dollar" than those struck in 1975 (but still dual-dated 1776-1976).

Type I.

Type II.

Coins with the earlier, fatter letters are referred to as Type I; those with the later, thinner letters are referred to as Type II. The Type I examples sell for slightly more at shops and shows.

The 40-percent-silver versions do not have the design variation.

Where's the show?

There's a coin show just about every weekend somewhere in the country. They range from mega-events, such as the American Numismatic Association's annual gatherings, to smaller one-day shows sponsored by a local coin club.

Coins *magazine.*

To find a show near you, check the community events listings in your local newspaper. Or, pick up a copy of the monthly *Coins* magazine (available on most newsstands) or weekly *Numismatic News*. Each lists upcoming shows of all sizes held throughout the country.

Chapter 5
Collecting the 50 State Quarters

The 50 State Quarters program is the most successful mass collecting opportunity in U.S. Mint history. The Mint estimates that 147 million people collect the coins. In addition, the program has generated billions of dollars in revenue, which has gone toward reduction of the national debt.

The story behind the coin

President Bill Clinton signed the 50 States Commemorative Coin Program Act into law on Dec. 1, 1997. The bill originated in the Senate. It was introduced to "honor the unique Federal republic of 50 States that comprise the United States" and to "promote the diffusion of knowledge among the youth of the United States about the individual States, their history and geography, and the rich diversity of the national heritage."

The bill provided that from 1999 through 2008, the quarter's reverse would be redesigned to honor each of the 50 states. Five new designs would be introduced each year, and each new design would honor a different state. The states would be honored in the order in which they ratified the Constitution or were admitted to the union.

The bill gave authority for final approval of the designs to the Treasury secretary. It required the secretary to consult with each state's governor or the governor's designee on the respective state's design. The designs were also reviewed by the U.S. Mint, the Citizens Coinage Advisory Committee,

and the Commission of Fine Arts before the secretary's final approval.

The law banned any "frivolous or inappropriate" design. It further prohibited the depiction of a head-and-shoulders bust of any person, living or dead, or any representation of a living person.

To accommodate the reverse designs, the words "United States of America" were moved from the quarter's reverse to its obverse, and the date was moved from the obverse to the reverse.

The law also authorized the Mint to produce uncirculated and proof examples of the 50 State Quarters for sale to collectors and to produce examples in 90-percent-silver composition for sale to collectors.

Mintmarks

Circulation strikes of the 50 State Quarters were produced at the Philadelphia ("P" mintmark) and Denver ("D" mintmark) mints. Thus, 100 coins—a "P" and "D" example of each state—are required to complete a set of circulating 50 State Quarters.

Special collector versions—for inclusion in mint and proof sets, and the 90-percent-silver examples—were produced by the San Francisco Mint and carry an "S" mintmark.

The mintmark on 50 State Quarters is located on the obverse behind the bow in Washington's hair and below the words "In God We Trust." It is approximately the same location for the mintmark on quarters used since 1968.

Where to get them

A close watch on pocket change can quickly fill holes in a 50 State Quarters folder and may be the most fun way to collect the series. One collector filled about half of the 100 holes in his folder in about a year's time just from pocket change.

A year of searching pocket change filled about half of the holes in this 50 State Quarters folder.

If you find a duplicate of a coin already in your folder, keep the one in better condition.

Searching rolls or other sources of bulk change can again speed the process. Five rolls of quarters (200 coins total) obtained from a local bank yielded the 50 State Quarters listed in the chart on page 62. Not counting duplicates (indicated in parenthesis), the sample rolls produced 47 of the 100 coins needed to complete a set of circulation strikes.

Nice examples of 50 State Quarters are also available individually at coin shops and shows for a small premium.

50 State Quarters found in five rolls of quarters
Numbers in parenthesis indicates total number found.

Date	Mintmark	State
1999	P	Connecticut
1999	D	Connecticut (2)
1999	D	Delaware
1999	D	New Jersey
1999	D	Pennsylvania (2)
2000	D	Maryland (2)
2000	D	Massachusetts
2000	P	Massachusetts
2000	D	New Hampshire
2000	P	New Hampshire (2)
2000	D	South Carolina (4)
2000	P	Virginia (4)
2001	D	Kentucky
2001	P	New York
2001	D	New York (5)
2001	D	Rhode Island (2)
2001	D	Vermont
2002	P	Indiana (3)
2002	P	Louisiana
2002	D	Louisiana (2)
2002	D	Mississippi (3)
2003	D	Alabama
2003	P	Alabama

Date	Mintmark	State
2003	D	Arkansas
2003	P	Arkansas
2003	P	Illinois
2004	D	Iowa (3)
2004	D	Michigan (2)
2004	D	Texas
2004	P	Texas
2004	D	Wisconsin
2005	P	Kansas
2005	P	Minnesota
2005	D	Minnesota (2)
2005	P	Oregon
2005	D	West Virginia (2)
2005	P	West Virginia (2)
2006	D	Colorado (4)
2006	P	Nevada
2006	D	Nevada (3)
2006	D	North Dakota (3)
2006	D	South Dakota (2)
2007	D	Idaho (2)
2007	D	Montana (3)
2007	D	Utah
2007	D	Washington (2)
2007	D	Wyoming

Condition

On the obverse, Washington's cheek and the hair around his ear remain key points to check for wear on 50 State Quarters. Because of the wide variety of designs, it is difficult to pinpoint specific areas to check on reverses. In general, check detailed areas in the designs and look for a minimum of scratches and other surface abrasions.

How to store them

Folders provide adequate, inexpensive, and handy storage for 50 State Quarters collected from circulation. For coins purchased from a shop or show, 2-by-2 holders or an album in which both sides of the coin are protected are recommended. Follow all the rules for safe handling of coins (see Chapter 1) when transferring purchased coins from one storage method to another.

50 State Quarters specs

Clad composition

Diameter: 24.3 millimeters.

Weight: 5.67 grams.

Composition: Clad layers of 75-percent copper and 25-percent nickel bonded to a pure-copper core.

Silver composition

Diameter: 24.3 millimeters.

Weight: 6.25 grams.

Composition: 90-percent silver, 10-percent copper.

Total silver weight: 0.1808 troy ounces.

50 State Quarters release dates

Year	Date	State
1999	January 4	Delaware
1999	March 8	Pennsylvania
1999	May 17	New Jersey
1999	July 19	Georgia
1999	October 12	Connecticut
2000	January 3	Massachusetts
2000	March 13	Maryland
2000	May 22	South Carolina
2000	August 7	New Hampshire
2000	October 16	Virginia
2001	January 2	New York
2001	March 12	North Carolina
2001	May 21	Rhode Island
2001	August 6	Vermont
2001	October 15	Kentucky
2002	January 2	Tennessee
2002	March 11	Ohio
2002	May 20	Louisiana
2002	August 2	Indiana
2002	October 15	Mississippi
2003	January 2	Illinois
2003	March 17	Alabama
2003	June 2	Maine

Year	Date	State
2003	August 4	Missouri
2003	October 20	Arkansas
2004	January 26	Michigan
2004	March 29	Florida
2004	June 1	Texas
2004	August 30	Iowa
2004	October 25	Wisconsin
2005	January 31	California
2005	April 4	Minnesota
2005	June 6	Oregon
2005	August 29	Kansas
2005	October 14	West Virginia
2006	January 31	Nevada
2006	April 3	Nebraska
2006	June 14	Colorado
2006	August 28	North Dakota
2006	November 6	South Dakota
2007	January 29	Montana
2007	April 2	Washington

Year	Date	State
2007	August 3	Idaho
2007	September 3	Wyoming
2007	November 5	Utah
2008	January 28	Oklahoma
2008	April 7	New Mexico
2008	June 2	Arizona
2008	August 25	Alaska
2008	November 3	Hawaii

But wait! There's more!

Although the 50 State Quarters program was completed in 2008, collectors can watch for six more special quarters dated 2009. The 2009 issues honor the District of Columbia and the five U.S. territories: the Commonwealth of Puerto Rico, Guam, American Samoa, the U.S. Virgin Islands, and the Commonwealth of the Northern Mariana Islands.

The coins were scheduled for 2009 release in the order listed above. Like the 50 State Quarters, the obverses carry the traditional image of Washington and the reverses carry designs emblematic of the district or respective territory. The design selection process was similar to the process for the state quarters.

Also, like the 50 State Quarters, the U.S. Mint was scheduled to strike and sell special collector versions for inclusion in mint and proof sets, and in the 90-percent-silver composition.

"50 State Quarters," officially

The term "50 State Quarters" is a registered trademark of the U.S. Mint.

What if a state had been added?

What if the nation had added a state during the 10-year 50 State Quarters program? The 1997 authorizing law provided that the Treasury secretary could have ordered the striking of an additional quarter to honor the new state during any year in the 10-year program.

Chapter 6
Collecting Franklin Half Dollars

1953 Franklin half dollar.

Franklin half dollars are an excellent choice for collectors looking to take the next step after collecting coins from circulation. They offer many virtues as a first series to collect through buying:

- Most of the issues in the series are now more than 50 years old.
- They were struck in the traditional 90-percent-silver composition and contain more than a third of an ounce of precious metal.
- They are big, making them easy to examine and grade.
- Examples are readily available at shows, shops, and through advertisements in coin-collecting publications.
- The series is long (1948-1963), making for a significant accomplishment when a collection is completed. But it is not so long that completing it is excessively challenging.
- Nice examples in higher circulated grades or even lower uncirculated grades are affordable.

The story behind the coin

Mint Director Nellie Tayloe Ross was apparently the driving force behind the change from the Walking Liberty half dollar to the Franklin half dollar in 1948. Some collectors may consider the switch an artistic faux pas. Adolph A. Weinman's Walking Liberty design is considered a classic in U.S. coinage

history. John R. Sinnock's staid bust of
Franklin is technically sound but not as
aesthetically pleasing.

Ross, however, wanted to introduce
a coin honoring Benjamin Franklin for
some time. A U.S. Mint news release (dated
Jan. 7, 1948) announcing the new coin says,
"Mrs. Ross envisaged several years ago a new
half dollar honoring Franklin and the Liberty
Bell."

Only the Treasury secretary had to
approve the design changes because the
Walking Liberty half dollar, introduced in
1916, had been used for more than 25 years.

*The Walking Liberty
half dollar preceded the
Franklin half dollar.*

According to some historical accounts,
Ross also considered changing the
cent's design to depict Franklin
because of his saying "A penny
saved is twopence clear," which
evolved into "A penny saved is a
penny earned." But she chose the
half dollar instead because the
larger silver coin allowed for a
better image of Franklin.

Sinnock's bust of Franklin on
the obverse is a "composite study
of Franklin's face in full profile,"
the Mint's 1948 news release
says. It was based on a variety of
Franklin portraits, the Mint said.
The Liberty Bell depiction on the
reverse is based on the 1926 U.S.

*Most Franklin half dollars sell for
about $10 each in nice circulated
or lower uncirculated grades.*

Sesquicentennial commemorative half dollar, also designed by Sinnock.

Where to get them

It's possible a well-worn Franklin half dollar could still turn up in a roll of half dollars or another source for bulk change. But the chances that the big coin in a denomination that isn't popular in circulation could get through without being put aside at some point are slim.

Thus, coin shops, shows, and advertisements in coin-collecting publications are the best sources for collectible Franklin half dollars. They are commonly found through all three.

How much?

Expect to pay about $10 per coin for Franklin half dollars in upper circulated or lower uncirculated grades. Some key dates may be higher. They include the 1949-D, 1949-S, 1952-S, and 1955.

Franklin half dollars in upper uncirculated grades can sell for hundreds or even thousands of dollars. The book "U.S. Coin Digest" lists the 1953-S in grade MS-65 with full lines on the lower part of the Liberty Bell at $16,000.

Mintmarks

Franklin half dollars have either no mintmark, indicating they were struck at the Philadelphia Mint; a "D" mintmark for Denver; or an "S" mintmark for San Francisco. The "S" mintmark was used in only five years: 1949 and 1951-1954.

The mintmark on Franklin half dollars is located on the reverse.

The mintmark appears on the reverse, above the wooden beam holding the Liberty Bell.

Condition

On the obverse, the high point of Franklin's cheek and the hair around his ear are key areas to check for wear. On the reverse, check the straps holding the bell to the beam and the lettering on the bell itself.

Uncirculated examples with full lines running across the bottom of the bell command substantial premiums. These are often listed as "MS-65FBL" in value guides, meaning a coin grading MS-65 with "full bell lines."

How to store them

Franklin half dollars purchased through shows, shops, or advertisements should be stored in 2-by-2 holders or an album that protects both sides of the coin. When it's necessary to handle a coin outside of a holder, follow all the rules outlined in Chapter 1 for safe handling of coins.

Franklin half dollar specs

Designer: John R. Sinnock.
Diameter: 30.6 millimeters.
Weight: 12.5 grams.
Composition: 90-percent silver, 10-percent copper.
Total silver weight: 0.3618 troy ounces.

1962 proof Franklin half dollar.

Death of an engraver

John Sinnock, the Mint engraver who designed the Franklin half dollar, never saw his Franklin design on a production coin. Sinnock died in 1947, after completing work on the design but before production of the coin began.

Franklin half dollar checklist

_____ 1948	_____ 1954-S
_____ 1948-D	_____ 1955
_____ 1949	_____ 1956
_____ 1949-D	_____ 1957
_____ 1949-S	_____ 1957-D
_____ 1950	_____ 1958
_____ 1950-D	_____ 1958-D
_____ 1951	_____ 1959
_____ 1951-D	_____ 1959-D
_____ 1951-S	_____ 1960
_____ 1952	_____ 1960-D
_____ 1952-D	_____ 1961
_____ 1952-S	_____ 1961-D
_____ 1953	_____ 1962
_____ 1953-D	_____ 1962-D
_____ 1953-S	_____ 1963
_____ 1954	_____ 1963-D
_____ 1954-D	

The better bird

Federal law requires a depiction of an eagle on circulating coins with a value of 25 cents or more, so a small eagle was added to the right of the Liberty Bell on the Franklin half dollar reverse to satisfy the provision. Benjamin Franklin would probably have liked the eagle's limited role in the design. He considered it a bird of "bad moral character" and favored instead the turkey, which he called a "true original Native of America," as a national symbol.

The what half dollar?

Some value guides may list a 1955 "Bugs Bunny" Franklin half dollar. An obverse die was damaged in coin production that year, apparently when it was struck in the coining press by a reverse die without a blank coin in between.

As subsequent coins were struck by the damaged die, Franklin's upper lip was split, giving him the appearance of having large front teeth like the cartoon character for which the variety is nicknamed.

The variety sells for a slight premium over regular 1955 Franklin half dollars but is not required for a collection of the series to be regarded as complete.

What's a troy ounce?

Silver and gold are weighed in troy ounces. A troy ounce (31.103 grams) is slightly heavier than an avoirdupois ounce (28.350 grams). Twelve troy ounces equal one troy pound.

The term originated in the city of Troyes, France, whose medieval fairs set the standards for European weights and measures.

Chapter 7
Collecting
Kennedy Half Dollars

Now in its fifth decade, the
Kennedy half dollar series spans several
milestones in U.S. coinage history:
- The first issues, dated 1964,
  were struck in the traditional 90-
  percent-silver composition.
- From 1965 through 1970, they
  were struck in a 40-percent-silver
  composition that is unique among
  circulating U.S. coins.
- Since 1971, they have been struck in the
  copper-nickel clad composition used
  for other circulating U.S. coins.

*Kennedy half dollars
were introduced in 1964.*

- As noted in Chapter 4, the Kennedy
  half dollar was also part of the Bicentennial coinage
  series struck in 1975 and 1976 with special reverses and
  the dual dates "1776-1976."

The story behind the coin

It was only days after John F. Kennedy's assassination on
Nov. 22, 1963, when proposals to honor the slain president on
a coin emerged. The quarter, half dollar, and dollar were all
considered before the half dollar was chosen.

President Lyndon Johnson announced his support for
honoring Kennedy on the half dollar in a news release on Dec.
10, 1963. Congressional approval was required because the
Franklin half dollar design had been used for less than 25 years.

Johnson and many in Congress wanted the new coin approved quickly so production could begin with the new year's coinage in January 1964. That would avoid having half dollars of two different designs (Franklin and Kennedy) struck in the same year and thus avoid the added expense of having to prepare dies for two different designs in the same year.

Congressional approval did indeed come quickly. Johnson signed the bill authorizing the Kennedy half dollar on Dec. 30, 1963.

U.S. Mint documents, however, reveal that Mint engravers were advised of a probable Kennedy coin as early as late November 1963. The Mint's chief engraver, Gilroy Roberts, said Mint Director Eva Adams notified him of the probable change "shortly after" Kennedy's assassination. "A day or so later, about November 27th, Miss Adams called again and informed me that the Half dollar had been chosen for the new design," Roberts said in his written recollection of the time. Roberts further related that the president's widow, Jacqueline Kennedy, did not want to replace the image of George Washington on the quarter with her late husband's image.

Design of the Kennedy half dollar was based on his official U.S. Mint presidential medal.

Thus, work on the Kennedy half dollar began at the Mint before the authorizing legislation was signed into law. To accommodate the tight turnaround time from concept to production, it was decided to adapt artwork already in-house.

Kennedy's portrait on the obverse and the presidential seal on the reverse were both based on his official presidential medal. Roberts had designed the medal's obverse, so he worked on adapting it for the half dollar. His assistant engraver, Frank Gasparro, who later succeeded Roberts as chief engraver, had designed the medal's reverse, so he worked on adapting it for the half dollar.

They apparently worked quickly, because trial strikes were made December 13, more than two weeks before President Johnson signed the authorizing legislation. Regular production of the Kennedy half dollar began simultaneously at the Philadelphia and Denver mints at 11 a.m. Eastern time on Feb. 11, 1964.

Adams expected the two mints combined to strike 90 million Kennedy half dollars in 1964, about the same number of Franklin half dollars struck in 1963. But demand for the new coin was so great that 1964 production at the two mints combined topped 433 million.

1964 Kennedy half dollars sell for $5 to $10 in lower uncirculated grades.

Where to get them

Several strategies can be used to collect Kennedy half dollars because of their long run and the aforementioned variety in composition. Collectors, therefore, may want to focus on just one segment of the series at a time. When that segment is complete, they can move on to another.

Following is a series breakdown:

1964

It's possible that a 1964 Kennedy half dollar may still turn up in pocket change or rolls, but the chances of one of the 90-percent-silver coins going undetected through circulation all these years are small. Thus, shops and shows are the best bets for acquiring one. Expect to pay about $5 to $10 for a nice example in a lower uncirculated grade.

1965-1970

The 40-percent-silver issues may have a slightly better chance of slipping through in circulation, but five rolls of half dollars (100 coins) obtained from a local bank yielded none. So shows and shops are the places to go again. About $5 each should buy pleasing examples in lower circulated grades.

1965-1970 Kennedy half dollars sell for about $5 each in lower circulated grades.

1971-date

Circulating coinage—be it pocket change, rolls from banks, or other sources of bulk change—is a good source for circulated examples of these base-metal issues. Coins from the five-roll sample mentioned above filled 20 of 35 holes in a Whitman folder for half dollars dated 1964 through 1985. The oldest was a 1971-D.

Look to shows or shops for better examples in lower uncirculated grades, especially for the older issues. Expect to pay $1 to $2 apiece.

Mintmarks

Kennedy half dollars with no mintmark were struck at the Philadelphia Mint. A "P" mintmark began appearing on Philadelphia

The mintmark on 1964 Kennedy half dollars appears on the reverse.

strikes in 1980. A "D" mintmark indicates the Denver Mint. Proofs and other special versions struck specially for sale directly to collectors through the years were struck at the San Francisco Mint and carry an "S" mintmark.

Since 1968, the mintmark on Kennedy half dollars has appeared on the obverse.

On 1964 Kennedy half dollars, the mintmark is located on the reverse below the eagle's right claw. From 1968 to the present, it is located on the obverse between Kennedy's neck and the date.

Condition

Kennedy's cheek and hair are key points to check for wear on the obverse. In particular, check for detail in the hair between the part in Kennedy's hair and his ear. On the reverse, the eagle's tail feathers are key points.

How to store them

Folders for Kennedy half dollars are available and provide adequate storage for coins collected from circulation. Uncirculated coins—those purchased at shows or shops—should be stored in 2-by-2 holders or albums in which both sides of the coin are protected. If it is necessary to handle an uncirculated Kennedy half dollar, follow the rules for safe handling of coins outlined in Chapter 1.

A search of five rolls filled 20 of the 35 holes in a Kennedy half dollar folder.

Kennedy half dollar specs

Obverse designer: Gilroy Roberts.
Reverse designer: Frank Gasparro.
Diameter: 30.6 millimeters.

1964

Weight: 12.5 grams.
Composition: 90-percent silver, 10-percent copper.
Total silver weight: 0.3618 troy ounces.

1965-1970

Weight: 11.5 grams.
Composition: clad layers of 80-percent silver and 20-percent copper bonded to a core of 20.9-percent silver and 79.1-percent copper.
Total silver weight: 0.148 troy ounces.

1971-date

Weight: 11.34 grams.
Composition: clad layers of 75-percent copper and 25-percent nickel bonded to a pure-copper core.

Kennedy half dollar checklist

Circulation strikes

_____ 1964
_____ 1964-D
_____ 1965
_____ 1966
_____ 1967
_____ 1968-D
_____ 1969-D
_____ 1971
_____ 1971-D

2004-S proof Kennedy half dollar.

_____ 1972	_____ 1989-P
_____ 1972-D	_____ 1989-D
_____ 1973	_____ 1990-P
_____ 1973-D	_____ 1990-D
_____ 1974	_____ 1991-P
_____ 1974-D	_____ 1991-D
_____ 1976	_____ 1992-P
_____ 1976-D	_____ 1992-D
_____ 1977	_____ 1993-P
_____ 1977-D	_____ 1993-D
_____ 1978	_____ 1994-P
_____ 1978-D	_____ 1994-D
_____ 1979	_____ 1995-P
_____ 1979-D	_____ 1995-D
_____ 1980-P	_____ 1996-P
_____ 1980-D	_____ 1996-D
_____ 1981-P	_____ 1997-P
_____ 1981-D	_____ 1997-D
_____ 1982-P	_____ 1998-P
_____ 1982-D	_____ 1998-D
_____ 1983-P	_____ 1999-P
_____ 1983-D	_____ 1999-D
_____ 1984-P	_____ 2000-P
_____ 1984-D	_____ 2000-D
_____ 1985-P	_____ 2001-P
_____ 1985-D	_____ 2001-D
_____ 1986-P	_____ 2002-P
_____ 1986-D	_____ 2002-D
_____ 1987-P	_____ 2003-P
_____ 1987-D	_____ 2003-D
_____ 1988-P	_____ 2004-P
_____ 1988-D	_____ 2004-D

_____ 2005-P   _____ 2007-D
_____ 2005-D   _____ 2008-P
_____ 2006-P   _____ 2008-D
_____ 2006-D   Series is ongoing.
_____ 2007-P

The president's widow approves

Among those who reviewed the Kennedy half dollar design before it entered production was the president's widow, Jacqueline Kennedy. "Mrs. Kennedy was favorably impressed with the design on both sides of the coin," Mint chief engraver Gilroy Roberts later recalled, "but felt it would be an improvement if the part in the hair, on the portrait, was less pronounced and more accents were added."

Roberts said the suggested changes were made before production began.

"They also had in mind a design showing a full figure or half figure of the late President," Roberts said. "There was simply not enough time to create new designs and medals, get approvals, etc. and have the new coin in production by January, 1964. I strongly advocated the simplicity and directness of a profile portrait as being the best possible arrangement for a handsome, outstanding coin whose beauty would endure and there could be no doubt as to the identity of the subject."

Why no 1970 half dollars?

In 1970 the U.S. Mint struck Kennedy half dollars for inclusion in mint sets and proof sets only. None were struck for circulation.

The 40-percent-silver half dollars struck for circulation from 1965 through 1969 were the only U.S. precious-metal coins remaining in circulation. The public hoarded them, resulting in chronic shortages of the denomination.

The Mint suspended circulation production of the half dollar for 1970 until Congress authorized a change to the clad composition used for the circulating dime and quarter.

The 1970 half dollars struck for mint sets that year were produced at Denver and have a "D" mintmark. The proof versions were struck at San Francisco and have an "S" mintmark.

1970-D (left) and 1970-S Kennedy half dollars.

Why no 1975 half dollars?

Kennedy half dollars struck in 1975 and 1976 carried the special Bicentennial reverse design and were all dated "1776-1976."

The silver half lives on

In 1992 the U.S. Mint resumed production of the traditional 90-percent-silver half dollars, but they are included in annual mint and proof sets only, not for circulation. All are produced at the San Francisco Mint and have an "S" mintmark.

Collectors can purchase current-year sets directly from the Mint. Sets from previous years are available on the secondary market, such as coin shops and shows.

1998-S silver Kennedy half dollar.

Chapter 8
Collecting Eisenhower Dollars

The Eisenhower dollar continued the 20th-century trend of honoring deceased presidents on coins. It is the last of the large (38.1 millimeters in diameter) dollar coins, but unfortunately for the former World War II general, and later president, the denomination and size have never been popular for a circulating coin. Thus, the series was short-lived (1971-1978).

Collectors today, however, still value the series for its subject and the very bulk that made it unpopular in circulation. Its short run also makes it an easy and affordable series to complete. Some special collector issues struck in silver are an optional bonus to a collection of "Ike dollars," as they are commonly called in the hobby.

1971-D Eisenhower dollar.

The story behind the coin

Dwight D. Eisenhower, supreme commander of the Allied forces in Europe during World War II and the 34th U.S. president, died March 28, 1969. Legislation to again strike a dollar coin, which had not been produced since 1935, was introduced in Congress the following fall. It stated that Eisenhower be honored on the dollar's obverse. The reverse was to be emblematic of the first moon landing, which occurred July 20, 1969.

Honoring Eisenhower apparently wasn't the sole motivation for the legislation. Several historical accounts say Nevada casino interests pushed for the United States to again strike a dollar coin.

The legislation did not become law until Dec. 31, 1970. But like the Kennedy half dollar, U.S. Mint engravers began work on the new coin's design well before the legislation was approved.

Mint chief sculptor and engraver Frank Gasparro designed both sides of the coin. He started work on the obverse in spring 1969 and on the reverse the following fall.

Mint documents say Gasparro's obverse design was inspired by his attendance at a welcome-home and victory parade in Eisenhower's honor on June 20, 1945, in New York City. Then a junior engraver at the Mint, Gasparro had a curbside view of the parade on Fifth Avenue.

"Mr. Gasparro got only a fleeting glimpse of the Supreme Commander of the Allied Armies in Europe as he rode by," the Mint documents say. "He carried his image of Eisenhower's courage and character back to work with him at the Philadelphia Mint and immediately made a profile drawing suitable to cut directly in steel and capture the strong facial features that so deeply impressed him."

Twenty-four years later, Gasparro referred back to his 1945 drawings and other Eisenhower portraits when he began work on the dollar coin.

For the reverse, Gasparro fashioned an eagle with an olive branch, a symbol of peace, in its claws landing on the moon with the Earth symbolized as a small orb in the background. The Apollo 11 spacecraft that first landed on the moon was nicknamed "The Eagle."

Trial strikes were made Jan. 21, 1971, at the Philadelphia

Mint, but circulation production did not begin until late fall of that year. All circulation coins were struck in the clad composition.

The Eisenhower dollar legislation also authorized the production of 40-percent-silver specimens for inclusion in mint and proof sets. Production of these special collector versions began March 31, 1971, at the San Francisco Mint. The 40-percent-silver Ike dollars were also produced from 1972 through 1974 in uncirculated and proof versions and again in 1975 and 1976 with the Bicentennial reverse.

Where to get them

Because of their obsolete size, Eisenhower dollars rarely turn up in circulation. A bank here or there may still have a rare roll of them or other small supply stuck in a drawer somewhere. Like the Kennedy half dollars, the coins were also hoarded by some when new, so an individual stash or two may surface also.

Ike dollars, however, are commonly found at shows and shops, which are the best sources for completing a collection of nice examples.

1974-D Eisenhower dollar.

How much?

Expect to pay $3 to $5 for a nice uncirculated example of a circulation strike in the clad composition. Exceptions are the 1973 and 1973-D, which have mintages of only two million each. (The next lowest mintage among circulation strikes is the 1974 at 27.3 million.) Expect to pay $10 to $15 for either of the 1973 circulation versions.

The 40-percent-silver versions of 1971-1974 are slightly more—$5 to $10 for those originally issued in mint sets. According to the book "U.S. Coin Digest," the proof versions of the same years range up to $35. The 1973-S proof is the most expensive.

Mintmarks

Circulating Eisenhower dollars have either no mintmark, indicating they were struck at Philadelphia, or a "D" mintmark for Denver. The 40-percent-silver versions were struck at San Francisco and have an "S" mintmark.

The mintmark appears on the obverse below Eisenhower's neck and above the date.

Condition

High points on the obverse to check for wear are Eisenhower's cheekbone and jaw line. On the reverse, check for detail in the eagle's head and wing feathers.

How to store them

Uncirculated and proof versions of Eisenhower dollars purchased at shops and shows should be stored in 2-by-2 holders or an album in which both sides of the coins are protected. Follow all the rules outlined in Chapter 1 for safe handling of coins.

Eisenhower dollar specs

Designer: Frank Gasparro.
Diameter: 38.1 millimeters.

Circulation strikes

Weight: 22.68 grams.
Composition: 75-percent copper and 25-percent nickel bonded to a pure copper core.

Mint sets and proof sets

Weight: 24.59 grams.

Composition: clad layers of 80-percent silver and 20-percent copper bonded to a core of 20.9-percent silver and 79.1-percent copper.

Total silver weight: 0.3161 troy ounces.

Checklist

Clad composition

_____ 1971

_____ 1971-D

_____ 1972

_____ 1972-D

_____ 1973

_____ 1973-D

_____ 1973-S (proofs only)

_____ 1974

_____ 1974-D

_____ 1974-S (proofs only)

_____ 1976

_____ 1976-D

_____ 1976-S (proofs only)

_____ 1977

_____ 1977-D

_____ 1977-S (proofs only)

_____ 1978

_____ 1978-D

_____ 1978-S (proofs only)

1972-S proof Eisenhower dollar.

40-percent-silver composition

Uncirculated versions were struck for inclusion in mint sets; proof versions were struck for inclusion in proof sets.

_____ 1971-S uncirculated	_____ 1973-S proof
_____ 1971-S proof	_____ 1974-S uncirculated
_____ 1972-S uncirculated	_____ 1974-S proof
_____ 1972-S proof	_____ 1976-S uncirculated
_____ 1973-S uncirculated	_____ 1976-S proof

A true silver dollar

Circulating dollar coins of clad composition are often referred to as "silver" dollars, but the term should be reserved for dollar coins that actually contain the precious metal.

The traditional silver dollars of the 1800s were composed of 90-percent silver and contain 0.7736 troy ounces of the precious metal. The last circulating U.S. silver dollar was struck in 1935.

The 40-percent-silver versions of the Eisenhower dollars, because they contain some of the precious metal, can truly be called silver dollars.

1921 silver dollar.

The clad-composition coins struck for circulation, however, should not be called silver dollars.

A "peaceful eagle"

According to U.S. Mint documents, Mint officials were concerned about the characterization of the eagle on the Eisenhower dollar's reverse. Mint Director Mary Brooks directed designer Frank Gasparro to fashion a "peaceful eagle." Gasparro described the resulting depiction as a "pleasant-looking eagle."

Mamie approved

As was the case with the Kennedy half dollar, the widow of the president depicted on the coin was allowed to review and approve the Eisenhower dollar before it entered production. The U.S. Mint reported that Mamie Eisenhower was "especially pleased with the portrait of her late husband."

Making money

In 1971, the San Francisco Mint's four coining presses could produce a total of 240,000 uncirculated Eisenhower dollars in an eight-hour shift.

Mint profile: San Francisco

The San Francisco Branch Mint was authorized in 1852 to bring coin production closer to bullion sources. Coinage commenced in 1854 but stopped in 1955. It resumed again in 1968, largely to produce proof and other special versions of coins for sale directly to collectors, such as the 40-percent-silver Eisenhower dollars. Over the years, San Francisco has produced a wide range of base-metal, silver, and gold coinage.

The current San Francisco Mint.

Chapter 9
Collecting Anthony Dollars

Much maligned and derided during its early years, the Anthony dollar today has some collectible value and even features a couple of scarce varieties. For the beginning collector, the series is short, can be collected from circulation, and is loaded with historical perspective both for its subject and its own checkered past.

1981 Anthony dollar.

The story behind the coin

Despite their popularity with collectors today, the traditional large dollar coin (38.1 millimeters in diameter) was never popular in circulation. The public preferred a thin, light dollar bill to the heavy, bulky dollar coin. Thus, the Eisenhower dollar in the traditional size (see Chapter 8) suffered the same commercial fate as its silver predecessors a century earlier.

The U.S. government attempted to reverse the public's rejection of circulating dollar coins when it authorized a new, smaller dollar coin (26.5 millimeters in diameter) in legislation signed into law by President Jimmy Carter on Oct. 10, 1978. The law specified that the coin's obverse honor 19th-century women's activist Susan B. Anthony (1820-1906).

U.S. Mint Chief Engraver Frank Gasparro designed the obverse profile of Anthony. It was based on an engraving of Anthony by G.E. Perine. The reverse adapted Gasparro's design of an eagle landing on the moon used on the Eisenhower dollar.

On paper, a smaller dollar coin makes sense. It costs more to produce than a dollar bill, but it lasts longer in circulation, thus saving the government money in the long run.

But in practice, the Anthony dollar initially suffered the same commercial fate as its larger predecessors. The major reason was its similarity in size to the quarter, which is 24.3 millimeters in diameter. The two were often confused, and people sometimes spent the dollar coin while believing they were spending a quarter.

This primary criticism possibly fueled other derisive comments about the coin's design. Characteristic of Gasparro, the design was technically sound, but simply put, some felt Anthony wasn't pretty enough to be put on a coin. These critics apparently ignored the fact that George Washington never won any beauty contests either. Years later, Gasparro told an interviewer that he "worked hard" on the Anthony dollar design and was dismayed by the criticism of it.

The new dollar coin was released into circulation on July 2, 1979, in Anthony's hometown of Rochester, N.Y. Through 1980, the U.S. Mint struck more than 847 million Anthony dollars, but by 1981, many of them sat in Mint storage because banks were not ordering them. Thus, the Mint struck 1981-dated Anthony dollars for mint and proof sets only and stopped production altogether after 1981.

In the 1990s, however, mass-transit organizations and the vending-machine industry started drawing down the government's inventory of Anthony dollars as their automated systems started accepting the higher denomination. On May 20, 1999, the Mint announced that it would strike 1999-dated Anthony dollars for circulation to meet demand until production of the new Sacagawea dollar coin could begin in 2000. The Mint struck more than 41 million 1999 Anthony dollars.

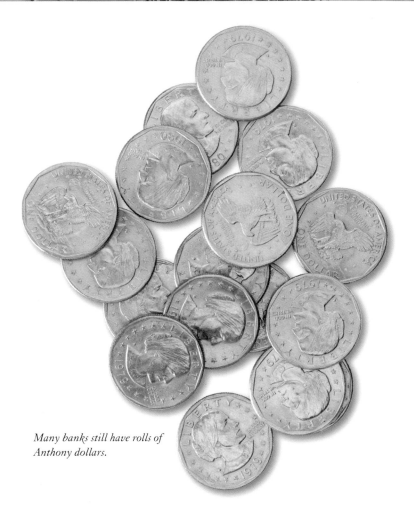

Many banks still have rolls of Anthony dollars.

Where to get them

Other than change from a vending machine, a dollar coin appears rarely in everyday cash transactions. Banks, however, still keep rolls of Anthony dollars in inventory and are the best bet for collecting examples from circulation. Uncirculated examples are also available at shops and shows.

A single roll of Anthony dollars (25 coins) obtained from a local bank yielded examples of all three mintmarks for 1979 and 1980. The only two circulation strikes missing from the roll were the 1999-P and 1999-D.

It also yielded a scarce variety of the 1979-P Anthony dollar. A slight design modification that year for the Philadelphia coins only resulted in the date being moved slightly closer to Anthony's collar and wider rims in the 11-sided border around the coin's design. It is commonly referred to as either the "near date" or "wide rim" variety.

A single roll of Anthony dollars yielded the scarce "near date" variety shown in the top photo. Compare its wider rims to the more common "far date" variety in the bottom photo.

In their book "Strike It Rich With Pocket Change," authors Brian Allen and Ken Potter value the coin at $8 in grade extra fine.

Mintmarks

Circulating Anthony dollars have either a "P" mintmark for Philadelphia, "D" mintmark for Denver, or an "S" mintmark for San Francisco. Proof versions with an "S" mintmark were also struck at San Francisco. The mintmark is located on the obverse just above Anthony's right shoulder.

Condition

Susan B. Anthony's cheekbone is a high point for wear on the obverse. Also check for detail in her hair and on her collar.

How to store them

Folders are fine for Anthony dollars collected from circulation. Uncirculated examples purchased at shows or shops should be stored in 2-by-2 holders or an album in which both sides of the coin are protected. The 1979-P "near date" or "wide rim" variety described earlier should also be stored in a 2-by-2 regardless of its source (circulation or purchased).

A single roll of Anthony dollars yielded all three mintmarks for 1979.

Anthony dollar specs

Designer: Frank Gasparro.

Diameter: 26.5 millimeters.

Weight: 8.1 grams.

Composition: clad layers of 75-percent copper and 25-percent nickel bonded to a pure-copper core.

Anthony dollar checklist

Circulation strikes

_____ 1979-P	_____ 1980-D
_____ 1979-D	_____ 1980-S
_____ 1979-S	_____ 1999-P
_____ 1980-P	_____ 1999-D

Anthony dollars dated 1981 were struck for mint ("P," "D," and "S" mintmarks) and proof ("S" mintmark) sets only and were not released into circulation. Proof versions of the 1979-S, 1980-S, and 1999-P were also struck.

The hendecagon coin

The original proposal for a smaller dollar coin called for it to be 11-sided, or a hendecagon, rather than round. But the vending-machine industry protested because the unique shape would not work in its machines. So the eventual Anthony dollar was made round with the hendecagon relegated to a border around the design to try to give the coin a visual and tactile characteristic different from the quarter.

Move over, Liberty

Susan B. Anthony was the first non-fictional woman to be depicted on a U.S. coin. Until the Lincoln cent was introduced in 1909, circulating U.S. coins featured either an allegorical representation of Liberty or images based on Native Americans.

Originally, Liberty was proposed for the new smaller dollar coin to be released in 1979, and U.S. Mint Chief Engraver Frank Gasparro prepared designs based on this proposal. His proposals emulated the depiction of Liberty on the first U.S. coins produced in quantity, in 1793. But Congress passed legislation mandating that Anthony be honored on the coin.

U.S. Mint Chief Engraver Frank Gasparro originally prepared a Liberty design for the first small dollar coin.

The Anthony proof varieties

Value guides list two types for the 1979 and 1981 proof Anthony dollars, produced at the San Francisco Mint. For each year, the Type I variety has a blob-like "S" mintmark. The Type II variety has a much clearer and more sharply defined "S" mintmark.

The Type II individual coins and sets are much more valuable than the Type I. A 1979 Type II proof Anthony dollar sells for a little over $100, and a 1981 Type II proof Anthony dollar sells for more than $200, according to the book "U.S. Coin Digest."

Type II 1979 and 1981 proof Anthony dollars have an "S" mintmark that is clearer than the blob-like Type I variety for each year (upper left).

Photos courtesy of James Wiles.

Chapter 10
Collecting Sacagawea Dollars

The Sacagawea dollar is yet another attempt to get U.S. consumers to use a circulating dollar coin. Its authorizing legislation attempted to correct the objections to the Anthony dollar. The coin has had mixed success in doing so since its introduction in 2000.

For collectors, the Sacagawea dollar offers an ongoing series with a pleasing design. Examples can be collected from circulation with a little bit of effort or purchased affordably, and the collection can be kept current as new dates are issued.

2007 Sacagawea dollar.

The story behind the coin

President Bill Clinton signed into law the U.S. Coin Act of 1997 on December 1 of that year. It mandated that a new golden-colored dollar coin be struck to replace the Anthony dollar.

The Sacagawea dollar has a plain edge (top) as opposed to the reeded edge used on the quarter.

Besides the color, the law also mandated that the coin have a "distinctive edge" as opposed to the reeded edge of the Anthony dollar and Washington quarter. It also has a wider border than other circulating coins. All of these features were incorporated into the new coin to try to distinguish it from the quarter and answer a major criticism of the Anthony dollar.

The law did not, however, mandate a design theme for the coin. That was left to Treasury Secretary Robert E. Rubin, who created the Dollar Coin Design Advisory Committee to lead the process. With public input, the citizen panel eventually recommended a design featuring Sacagawea, the Native American woman who accompanied Lewis and Clark on their exploration of the American West.

As the design selection process proceeded, U.S. Mint officials met quarterly with representatives from transit authorities, the vending-machine industry, the banking business, retail businesses, and others with an interest in the coin's success. All of this was an effort to make the new coin right where the old Anthony dollar went wrong.

The coin was released into commerce in January 2000. The following March, the Mint launched a marketing campaign, also mandated by the authorizing legislation, to increase awareness and promote acceptance of the new coin. The campaign cost $40 million, all of which came from Mint operating revenues, not tax dollars, according to the Mint.

Initially, it appeared the pre-production planning and marketing campaign paid off. The Mint said it produced and shipped more than 500 million Sacagawea dollars by the end of April 2000. In all, it produced more than 1.28 billion 2000-dated Sacagawea dollar coins for circulation.

By the following year, however, production fell to more than 133 million circulation strikes. From 2002 through

2007, circulation-strike production averaged just 7.36 million annually.

Besides any public bias against a dollar coin that may still linger, the Sacagawea dollar also faces competition as a circulating coin from the Presidential Dollar Coin Series, which began in 2007 and is scheduled to continue through 2016.

Where to get them

Despite the U.S. Mint's massive marketing campaign in the spring of 2000, dollar coins remain a rarity in pocket change. Thus, collectors seeking to assemble a set of circulation-strike Sacagawea dollars will have to expend some effort to acquire examples.

Local banks should have rolls of Sacagawea dollars, but finding a variety of date and mintmark combinations may be a problem.

Rolls from banks are again an option. A sample roll (25 coins) obtained from a local bank, however, contained all 2000-P examples, which have the highest mintage in the series so far at more than 767 million.

If you're a good customer at the bank and know a patient cashier, ask to see several rolls and try to check the date on the top coin in each roll. If possible, obtain rolls with different dates showing so you're assured of getting more than one date and mintmark combination.

The upside is that whatever rolls you do obtain should contain nice examples because the coins will have seen little or no circulation. The coins will have a certain number of scratches and marks from having been mass produced and shipped in large quantities, but there will be little to no actual wear on the coin because, unlike many circulating coins, they haven't been handled much.

Considering the effort required to find circulating examples, the best strategy for collecting Sacagawea dollars may be to simply buy nice uncirculated examples at shows or shops. Expect to pay $2 to $3 a coin; the 2006-D may be a bit more, according to *Coin Prices* magazine.

Mintmarks

Circulation-strike Sacagawea dollars have either a "P" mintmark for Philadelphia or a "D" mintmark for Denver. Proof versions are produced at San Francisco and have an "S" mintmark. The mintmark appears on the obverse below the date.

2000-P Sacagawea dollar.

Condition

On the obverse, check for wear on the high point of Sacagawea's cheekbone and for detail in her hair and her child's hair. On the reverse, check the highly detailed feathers on the eagle.

How to store them

Folders are available for Sacagawea dollar coins and are fine for coins collected from circulation. Many Sacagawea dollars, however, have seen little circulation and have little subsequent wear. So collectors may want to consider storage in which both sides of the coin are protected, such as 2-by-2 holders, even for examples collected from circulation.

Purchased coins should always be stored in albums in which both sides of the coin are protected, or in 2-by-2 or hard-plastic holders.

Sacagawea dollar specs

Obverse designer: Glenna Goodacre.
Reverse designer: Thomas D. Rogers Sr.
Diameter: 26.4 millimeters.
Weight: 8.07 grams.
Composition: 88.5-percent copper, six-percent zinc, 3.5-percent manganese, two-percent nickel.

Sacagawea dollar checklist

Circulation strikes

_____	2000-P	_____	2003-P
_____	2000-D	_____	2003-D
_____	2001-P	_____	2004-P
_____	2001-D	_____	2004-D
_____	2002-P	_____	2005-P
_____	2002-D	_____	2005-D

_____ 2006-P	_____ 2008-P
_____ 2006-D	_____ 2008-D
_____ 2007-P	Series is ongoing.
_____ 2007-D	

The sculptor's model

Sculptor Glenna Goodacre used a Shoshone college student, Randy'L Hedow Teton, as her model for the depiction of Sacagawea on the obverse of the golden dollar. The child Sacagawea is carrying on her back is a depiction of her son Jean Baptiste. Sacagawea was six months pregnant when she joined Lewis and Clark's expedition, and the child was born early in the journey. Goodacre also designed the Vietnam Women's Memorial in Washington, D.C.

Distinctive to the touch

Among the groups the U.S. Mint consulted before producing the Sacagawea dollar coin was the National Foundation for the Blind. Based on the foundation's input, the Mint gave the coin a smooth edge (instead of the quarter's reeded edge) and a wider rim to make it distinguishable by touch.

Cheerios coins

Cereal boxes have contained many trinkets over the years to try to entice buyers, especially kids. So the U.S. Mint turned to this traditional marketing gimmick when introducing the Sacagawea dollar.

During the coin's launch, Sacagawea dollars were inserted into 11 million boxes of General Mills' Cheerios. Buyers of the brand had a 1-in-2,000 chance of finding one of the coins in their purchased box.

"Advertising experts have estimated that the Cheerios campaign brought the Mint the equivalent of 132 million advertising impressions," the Mint reported in March 2001.

Hail to the chiefs

The U.S. Mint began issuing a series of circulating dollar coins honoring the first 38 U.S. presidents in 2007. Four different presidents will be honored in each year through 2015 in the order that they served. The final two—Richard M. Nixon and Gerald Ford—will be honored in 2016.

The coins will be struck in the same specifications as the Sacagawea dollar, which will continue to be struck for circulation.

See Chapter 26 for a complete listing of which presidents will be honored in which years.

Chapter 11
Collecting Modern U.S. Commemoratives

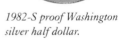

Congress has authorized a myriad of commemorative coin series since 1982.

Commemorative coins honor events, people, organizations, or other things, and are authorized by law. They are official U.S. government issues and legal tender, but they are not intended to circulate. Instead, the U.S. Mint—at a premium above face value—sells them directly to collectors. Laws authorizing commemorative coins usually mandate that a certain amount of the purchase price benefit a group or event related to the coin's theme.

1982-S proof Washington silver half dollar.

In terms of cost, collecting modern commemoratives is a step up from collecting coins from circulation at face value or buying them at shops or shows for a few dollars each. But focusing on one or more collecting strategies, as outlined earlier, can keep purchases within a budget.

The story behind the coins

The first U.S. commemorative coin was an 1892 half dollar for the Columbian Exposition. The exposition was held May 1-Oct. 30, 1893, in Chicago to commemorate the 400th anniversary of Columbus' arrival in the New World. The U.S. Mint struck 950,000 Columbian

1997-W proof Franklin Delano Roosevelt gold $5.

half dollars dated 1892 and more than 1.5 million dated 1893.

The Columbian half dollar opened the door to many other commemorative coins from the 1910s and continuing into the 1950s. Most were silver half dollars, but there was also an 1893 quarter (also for the Columbian Exposition), a number of gold dollars, two gold $2.50 coins, and two gold $50 coins.

The first U.S. commemorative coin: 1892 Columbian Exposition half dollar.

The coins were sold by the Mint at a premium above face value with a portion of the proceeds benefiting some organization or event related to the coin's theme. Some of the coins commemorated state anniversaries or national themes, such as the U.S. Sesquicentennial in 1926.

There were no less than 18 commemorative half dollars issued in 1936 alone. Among them was an issue commemorating the 75th anniversary of the Battle of Gettysburg. Others, however, were of little national importance, such as issues for the Cincinnati Music Center and the centennial of Elgin, Ill.

The proliferation of commemorative coins in the 1930s included a half dollar for the Cincinnati Music Center.

Congress grew weary of U.S. coinage being used as local fundraisers, and the flow of commemorative coins slowed in the 1940s and '50s. The last issue among what are commonly called "early" commemoratives was a 1954 half dollar honoring Booker T. Washington and George Washington Carver.

A 28-year hiatus on commemorative coinage ensued until Congress authorized a half dollar in the traditional 90-percent-silver composition to honor the 250th anniversary of George Washington's birth in 1982. Thus began what are commonly called "modern" commemoratives.

The Washington coin was a winner in many respects: First, its theme was of truly national significance and worthy of commemoration. Second, its design by Mint engraver Elizabeth Jones featured a striking depiction of Washington on horseback, a departure from the staid busts used for portraiture on coins since the Lincoln cent of 1909. The reverse, also designed by Jones, features a view of Washington's Mount Vernon home.

The last of the "early" commemoratives honored Booker T. Washington and George Washington Carver.

These factors, combined with the long break in commemorative coinage, made the coin popular with collectors. The Mint sold more than 2.2 million uncirculated versions ("D" mintmark) and almost 4.9 million proof versions ("S" mintmark).

Like the Columbian half dollar 90 years earlier, the George Washington half dollar opened the door to more commemorative coinage, and like the commemorative coinage of the 1930s, an undesirable proliferation resulted. The coins' themes in the 1990s weren't as localized as many of those in the 1930s, but commemorative coinage became an easy mark for senators and U.S. representatives looking to do a favor for a constituency or a favor for a fellow lawmaker by offering their vote for a commemorative coin program. Commemorative coins could raise funds for a pet cause through surcharges on the Mint's sales of the coins, and a vote for a program went largely unnoticed by the general public.

The year 1994 alone brought five commemorative coin programs: World Cup soccer, National Prisoner of War Museum, U.S. Capitol Bicentennial, Vietnam Veterans Memorial, and Women in Military Service Memorial. Although each theme had its virtues, the market for commemorative coins couldn't keep up with all the issues, and sales plummeted from the highs of the Washington half dollar and other early issues in the modern era.

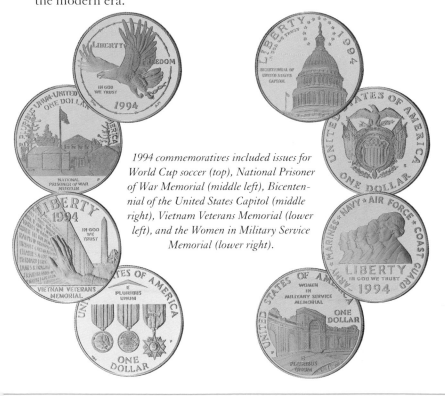

1994 commemoratives included issues for World Cup soccer (top), National Prisoner of War Memorial (middle left), Bicentennial of the United States Capitol (middle right), Vietnam Veterans Memorial (lower left), and the Women in Military Service Memorial (lower right).

In response, Congress passed the Commemorative Coin Reform Act of 1996. Among other provisions, it limits the number of commemorative themes to two per year. In addition, congressional proposals for commemorative coins must be reviewed by the Citizens Coinage Advisory Committee, which reports to the Treasury secretary. The 10-person committee consists of members from the general public and those with credentials in American history, sculpture, and numismatics.

Where to get them

Current-year commemoratives can be purchased directly from the U.S. Mint (www.usmint.gov). Issues from previous years can be purchased at shows, shops, or through advertisements in hobby publications, such as *Coins* magazine.

Collecting strategies

A complete collection of every commemorative half dollar, silver dollar, and gold coin issued since 1982 is a commendable but daunting goal for many collectors, especially beginners. Following

1996-P proof Atlanta Olympics silver dollar, high-jumper design.

are suggestions for getting started in collecting modern commemoratives, which can lead to expanding the collection in the future:

Collect what you like

If you see a modern commemorative coin and you like it, buy it. The coin may appeal to you because of its theme or design. Whatever the reason, if you like the coin and are willing to pay the asking price, it will make a great addition to your collection.

1988-W Olympiad gold $5.

By denomination

A new collector may want to focus on just the commemorative half dollars issued since 1982 or just the silver dollars. With a good value guide in hand and more money to spend, a new collector could also venture into gold coins and select one or more of the many commemorative gold $5 coins.

1993-S proof Thomas Jefferson silver dollar.

By theme

Collectors of modern commemoratives can also focus on a particular theme that appeals to them, such as presidents, the Olympics or other sports, women, or military themes. Again, collect what you like.

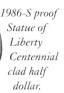

1990-P proof Eisenhower Centennial silver dollar.

As a complement to a circulating-coin collection

One or more commemorative coins can complement a collection of circulating coins with similar design themes. For example, a 1993 silver dollar commemorating the 250th anniversary of Thomas Jefferson's birth can complement a collection of Westward Journey nickels (see Chapter 3). A 1990 silver dollar commemorating the centennial of Dwight Eisenhower's birth can complement a collection of Eisenhower dollars (see Chapter 8).

1986-S proof Statue of Liberty Centennial clad half dollar.

By set

When selling a current-year commemorative series, the U.S. Mint often offers various sets containing individual coins in the series in uncirculated and proof versions. For example, the 1986 Statue of Liberty Centennial coin series consisted of a base-metal half dollar, silver dollar, and gold $5. Various sets of the series offered by the Mint that year included a two-coin set consisting of an uncirculated silver dollar and clad half dollar; a three-coin set consisting of uncirculated versions of each coin; and a six-coin set consisting of proof and uncirculated versions of each coin.

These and sets of other series can be found in their original Mint packaging at shops and shows, and through advertisements in hobby publications such as *Coins* magazine.

1986-S proof Statue of Liberty Centennial silver dollar.

1986-W proof Statue of Liberty Centennial gold $5.

How much?

Some of the least popular commemorative coins at the time of their issue are the most expensive on the secondary market today, and some of the most popular commemorative coins at the time of their issue are the most affordable today. Why? The least popular coins didn't sell as well, which resulted in lower mintages. Generally speaking, the scarcer coins are more valued by collectors, which increases demand and drives up their asking prices on the secondary market.

1996-S Atlanta Olympics clad half dollar, swimmer design.

For example, the 1982 George Washington silver commemorative half dollar was popular and sold well at the time of issue. With millions of coins produced, either an uncirculated or proof example can be purchased for under $10.

In contrast, less than 50,000 uncirculated versions of the 1996 Atlanta Olympics commemorative clad half dollar with the swimmer design were produced. Expect to pay more than $150 for one on the secondary market.

Coin Prices magazine, available on many newsstands, provides a complete list of modern U.S. commemorative coins and a guide to current retail values.

1993-S proof James Madison clad half dollar.

1991-S proof Mount Rushmore Golden Anniversary clad half dollar.

1989-S proof Bicentennial of the Congress silver dollar.

Mintmarks

Modern U.S. commemorative coins have either a "P" mintmark for Philadelphia, "D" for Denver, "S" for San Francisco, or a "W" for West Point, N.Y. Mintmark location varies by coin.

Condition

Commemorative coins are specially handled and packaged at the mints. Thus, grading is less of a factor in purchasing and collecting them.

1992-P proof Columbus Quincentenary silver dollar.

Still, check each coin before you purchase it or after you receive it in the mail. Make sure its surfaces are clean and free of scratches or other significant blemishes.

The U.S. Mint has a 30-day return policy for coins purchased directly from it. Mail-order dealers, such as those who advertise in *Coins* magazine, also offer return policies. Check individual ads for specific terms.

1995-S proof Civil War silver dollar.

How to store them

Keep commemorative coins in their original U.S. Mint packaging, whether purchased directly from the Mint or on the secondary market. The packaging is suitable for long-term storage and protects the coins from wear and blemishes that occur when handled directly.

Modern commemorative coin specs

Commemorative coins are struck in traditional specifications for the denomination and composition. Future issues may be subject to change from the specs listed.

1997-S proof Jackie Robinson silver dollar.

Clad half dollars

Diameter: 30.6 millimeters.

Weight: 11.34 grams.

Composition: clad layers of 75-percent copper and 25-percent nickel bonded to a pure-copper core.

Silver half dollars

Diameter: 30.6 millimeters.

Weight: 12.5 grams.

Composition: 90-percent silver, 10-percent copper.

Actual silver weight: 0.3618 troy ounces.

2004-P proof 125th Anniversary of the Light Bulb silver dollar.

Silver dollars

Diameter: 38.1 millimeters.

Weight: 26.73 grams.

Composition: 90-percent silver, 10-percent copper.

Actual silver weight: 0.76 troy ounces.

Gold $5

Diameter: 21.5 millimeters.

Weight: 8.359 grams.

Composition: 90-percent gold, 10-percent alloy.

Actual gold weight: 0.24 troy ounces.

Gold $10

1999 W proof George Washington gold $5.

Diameter: 27 millimeters.

Weight: 26.73 grams.

Composition: 90-percent gold, 10-percent alloy.

Actual gold weight: 0.484 troy ounces.

Checklist

All coins listed below were offered in proof and uncirculated versions.

Silver half dollars

_____ 1982 George Washington 250th Anniversary of Birth

_____ 1993 James Madison, Father of the Bill of Rights

Clad half dollars

_____ 1986 Statue of Liberty Centennial

_____ 1986 Bicentennial of the Congress

_____ 1991 Mount Rushmore Golden Anniversary

_____ 1991 World War II 50th Anniversary (struck in 1993)

_____ 1992 Olympics

_____ 1992 500th Anniversary of Columbus Discovery

_____ 1994 World Cup Soccer

_____ 1995 Atlanta Olympics (basketball design)

_____ 1995 Atlanta Olympics (baseball design)

_____ 1995 Civil War

_____ 1996 Atlanta Olympics (soccer design)

_____ 1996 Atlanta Olympics (swimmer design)

_____ 2001 U.S. Capitol

_____ 2003 First Flight Centennial

_____ 2008 Bald Eagle

Silver dollars

_____ 1983 Los Angeles XXII Olympiad

_____ 1984 Los Angeles XXII Olympiad

_____ 1986 Statue of Liberty Centennial

_____ 1987 The U.S. Constitution 200th Anniversary

_____ 1988 Olympiad

_____ 1989 Bicentennial of the Congress

_____ 1990 Eisenhower Centennial

_____ 1991 38th Anniversary Korea

_____ 1991 Mount Rushmore Golden Anniversary

_____ 1991 USO 50th Anniversary

_____ 1991-1995 World War II 50th Anniversary series (struck in 1993)

_____ 1992 Columbus Quincentenary

_____ 1992 Olympics

_____ 1992 The White House 1792-1992

_____ 1993 James Madison

_____ 1993 Thomas Jefferson 1743-1993

_____ 1994 National Prisoner of War Museum

_____ 1994 Bicentennial of United States Capitol

_____ 1994 Vietnam Veterans Memorial

_____ 1994 Women in Military Service Memorial

_____ 1994 World Cup '94

_____ 1995 Atlanta Olympics (gymnastics design)

_____ 1995 Atlanta Olympics (track and field design)

_____ 1995 Atlanta Olympics (cycling design)

_____ 1995 Atlanta Olympics (Paralympics design)

_____ 1995 Civil War

_____ 1995 Special Olympics World Games

_____ 1996 Atlanta Olympics (tennis design)

_____ 1996 Atlanta Olympics (rowing design)

_____ 1996 Atlanta Olympics (high-jumper design)

_____ 1996 Atlanta Olympics (Paralympics design)

_____ 1996 National Community Service

_____ 1996 Smithsonian Institution 1846-1996

_____ 1997 Jackie Robinson 50th Anniversary

_____ 1997 National Law Enforcement Officers Memorial

_____ 1997 United States Botanic Garden 1820-1995

_____ 1998 Black Revolutionary War Patriots

_____ 1998 Robert F. Kennedy

_____ 1999 Dolley Madison

_____ 1999 Yellowstone National Park

_____ 2000 Leif Ericson

_____ 2000 Library of Congress 1800-2000

_____ 2001 American Buffalo

_____ 2001 U.S. Capitol

_____ 2002 West Point Bicentennial

_____ 2002 XIX Olympic Winter Games

_____ 2003 First Flight Centennial

_____ 2004 125th Anniversary of the Light Bulb

_____ 2004 Lewis & Clark Bicentennial

_____ 2005 Chief Justice John Marshall

_____ 2005 Marines 1775-2005

_____ 2006 Benjamin Franklin Tercentenary (Franklin portrait design)

_____ 2006 Benjamin Franklin Tercentenary (kite-flying design)

_____ 2006 San Francisco Old Mint

_____ 2007 Founding of Jamestown 1607-2007

_____ 2007 Little Rock High School Desegregation

_____ 2008 Bald Eagle

2006-P proof Benjamin Franklin Tercentenary silver dollar, Franklin portrait design.

Gold $5

_____ 1986 Statue of Liberty Centennial

_____ 1987 Bicentennial of the Constitution

_____ 1988 Olympiad

_____ 1989 Bicentennial of the Congress

_____ 1991 Mount Rushmore Golden Anniversary

_____ 1991-1995 World War II 50th Anniversary (struck in 1993)

_____ 1992 Columbus Quincentenary

_____ 1992 Olympics

_____ 1993 James Madison
_____ 1994 World Cup '94
_____ 1995 Civil War
_____ 1995 Atlanta Olympics
(torch-runner design)
_____ 1995 Atlanta Olympics (stadium design)
_____ 1996 Atlanta Olympics (cauldron design)
_____ 1996 Atlanta Olympics (flag-bearer design)
_____ 1996 Smithsonian Institution 1846-1996
_____ 1997 Franklin Delano Roosevelt
_____ 1997 Jackie Robinson 50th Anniversary
_____ 1999 George Washington (bicentennial of death)
_____ 2001 U.S. Capitol
_____ 2002 XIX Olympic Winter Games
_____ 2006 San Francisco Old Mint
_____ 2007 Founding of Jamestown 1607-2007
_____ 2008 Bald Eagle

1993-W James Madison gold $5.

Gold $10
_____ 1984 Los Angeles XXII
Olympiad
_____ 2000 Library of Congress
_____ 2003 First Flight Centennial

2003-P proof First Flight Centennial gold $10.

Ancient roots
Commemoratives have their roots in some of the world's first coins. Roman generals used their coinage privileges to strike issues commemorating their military conquests.

Chapter 12
Collecting Mint and Proof Sets

Mint and proof sets have a long tradition in U.S. Mint history and among collectors. They were created as a means for collectors to obtain pristine examples of current-year coinage. That tradition continues today with a wide variety of sets available from the Mint, which reflects the wide variety of current U.S. coinage.

The story behind the coins

Proof coins are struck from specially selected, highly polished planchets and dies. They usually receive multiple strikes from the coining press at increased pressure. The result is a coin with mirror-like surfaces and, in recent years, a cameo effect on its raised design surfaces.

The coins are then carefully handled; placed in sealed, inert holders; and sold to collectors in sets. Traditionally, the sets contain one proof example of each coin struck for circulation that year (cent through dollar), but with the proliferation of commemorative coins and other special issues in recent years, such as the 50 State Quarters, the Mint has offered multiple proof sets in a single year.

In 2007, for example, the Mint's proof-set offerings included a Presidential dollar set; a set that contained 90-percent-silver examples of the dime, quarters, and half dollar; a 50 State Quarters set; and a 50 State Quarters silver set.

U.S. proof coins date back as early as 1795, but were struck largely as presentation pieces for VIPs. The Mint started selling sets to the general public in 1936. Proof sets were not produced from 1943 through 1949 and again from 1965 through 1967, but they have been offered continuously since 1968.

The U.S. Mint now offers multiple proof sets annually.

Like proof sets, mint sets have traditionally contained one example of each coin struck for circulation in their year of issue, including one example of each mintmark for a particular denomination. Unlike proof sets, however, the coins in mint sets are struck from production planchets and dies and do not receive multiple strikes from the coining press, so they look more like their circulating counterparts than high-quality proof coins do.

Annual mint sets traditionally *contain uncirculated examples of the year's circulating coinage.*

Coins in mint sets still receive special handling and packaging, so they are referred to as "uncirculated." They are sometimes removed from their original Mint packaging on the secondary market and sold individually. These account for the individual uncirculated examples of late-date coins sold at shows and shops.

The Mint has sold mint sets to the general public since 1947 with a couple of interruptions. From 1965-1967, the Mint did not produce proof sets or traditional mint sets. Instead it marketed what it called "Special Mint Sets." Coins in the Special Mint Sets were of higher quality than the traditional mint sets but were not up to proof-coin standards. The Mint did not offer mint sets in 1982 and 1983.

Where to get them

Current-year sets are available directly from the U.S. Mint (www.usmint.gov). Previous year's sets may be available directly from the Mint also if supplies last. For example, some 2007 sets were still available from the Mint in early 2008.

Past-year sets are available at shows, shops, or through advertisements in hobby publications such as *Coins* magazine. Some may also offer current-year sets.

How much?

In 2007, the U.S. Mint's prices on its various current-year proof and mint sets ranged from $13.95 to $44.95. On the secondary market, proof sets dating back to 1956 generally range from $5 to $60. Late-date mint sets generally range from $10 to $25.

Some scarcer sets may be higher. Consult a current copy of *Coin Prices* magazine, available on many newsstands, for a guide to current retail values for proof and mint sets.

Collecting strategies

A complete run of proof or mint sets from their first issues through the current year is not a practical goal for most collectors. Thus, many focus on a few particular years or series of years.

For example, some collectors seek sets from their birth year and the birth years of their family members. They may

Some collectors seek proof or mint sets from years with personal significance to them, such as birth or anniversary years.

also seek sets from other years that have significance to them, such as a wedding year.

Some may also focus on sets containing a particular commemorative or other series of coins. For example, some may seek a complete collection of proof 50 State Quarters.

Mintmarks

Proof coins from 1936 through 1964 were struck at the Philadelphia Mint and do not have mintmarks. The San Francisco Mint has produced proof coins for annual sets since 1968, and they are designated with an "S" mintmark.

1992-W proof Olympic (left) and 1993-W proof World War II gold $5 coins.

Proof modern commemoratives have been struck at all four mints (Philadelphia, Denver, San Francisco, and West Point, N.Y.) and may contain a "P," "D," "S," or "W" mintmark, depending on the individual issue.

2003-P proof First Flight Centennial silver dollar.

Annual mint sets have traditionally contained an example of each coin produced for circulation at each mint in the year of issue. So if quarters were produced at Philadelphia and Denver that year, the mint set would include an example of a Philadelphia-produced quarter (either no mintmark or a "P") and a Denver quarter ("D").

Condition

As noted, proof and mint sets are specially handled and packaged at the mints. Thus, grading is less of a factor in purchasing and collecting them.

2004-P proof Lewis and Clark silver dollar.

Still, check each coin in the set before you purchase it or after you receive it in the mail. Make sure the coins' surfaces are clean and free of scratches or other significant blemishes.

The U.S. Mint has a 30-day return policy for sets purchased directly from it. Mail-order dealers, such as those who advertise in *Coins* magazine, also offer return policies. Check individual ads for specific terms.

How to store them

As noted, proof and mint sets are sold by the U.S. Mint in sealed, inert holders and should be left in those holders for long-term storage. Mint sets from 1947 through 1958 were mounted in cardboard holders, which caused the coins to tarnish. Sets from those years will probably be found in some type of more secure aftermarket holder when offered on the secondary market.

Proof and mint set specs

The individual coins in proof and mint sets are struck to the same specifications as their circulating counterparts or, in the case of precious-metals coins, in the traditional specifications for a particular denomination in a particular metal.

Grading proof coins

Because proof coins are struck by a special process, they receive their own grading designation. A coin does not start out being a proof and then become mint state if it becomes worn or damaged. Once a proof coin, always a proof coin.

The American Numismatic Association's official standards for grading proof coins assign designations proof-60 through proof-70 (proof-61, proof-62, and so on) to these specially produced coins in various condition. The ANA says a proof coin with many marks, dents, scratches, or other blemishes should be called an "impaired" proof.

The non-Mint mint sets

In years when the U.S. Mint did not offer mint sets, some private companies compiled and marketed uncirculated sets. These privately produced and marketed sets still have collectible value depending on the scarcity and condition of their individual coins, but they should not be confused with the Mint's officially issued sets.

Chapter 13
Collecting Silver American Eagle Bullion Coins

Silver American Eagle bullion coins, and their gold counterparts, were historic firsts for the U.S. Mint when they made their debut in 1986. They were the first official U.S. coins struck primarily to be bought and sold for their bullion value. American Eagle bullion coins can be held in individual retirement accounts.

1992-S proof silver American Eagle bullion coin.

Some individual date and mintmark combinations, however, also have collectible numismatic value, including proof versions.

The story behind the coin

Gold and silver bullion coins, produced by various countries, are official government issues. They are legal tender, and usually have a nominal face value, but they are produced and sold as a convenient way for private citizens to invest in precious metals and are not intended to circulate. To facilitate their trade, the coins are sized based on their precious-metal content. Gold bullion coins, for example, usually contain either a tenth-ounce, quarter-ounce, half-ounce, or full troy ounce of gold. Silver bullion coins usually contain one troy ounce of precious metal.

The standard sizes and credibility of the issuing authority give investors and collectors confidence that when they buy one of the coins they are getting the stated amount of precious metal in the stated purity.

South Africa was the sole player in the bullion-coin market for a number of years. It introduced the Krugerrand, which contains one ounce of 0.917-fine gold, in 1967. Fractional versions of the Krugerrand (tenth-ounce through half-ounce) were introduced in 1980.

South Africa introduced its gold Krugerrand bullion coin in 1967.

Other countries followed with their own versions of bullion coins. Among the most popular are Canada's Maple Leaf, China's Panda, Great Britain's Britannia, and the Isle of Man's Angel. In 1986, the United States introduced its American Eagle series of gold and silver bullion coins, and they have also gained popularity in the market. A platinum Eagle was introduced in 1997.

The gold and platinum Eagles are offered in tenth-ounce, quarter-ounce, half-ounce, and one-troy-ounce versions. Silver Eagles are offered in just one size, which contains one troy ounce of 0.999-fine precious metal.

Gold American Eagle bullion coins are available in sizes ranging from a tenth-ounce (upper left) to one troy ounce (bottom).

The U.S. Mint adapted two classic coinage designs for the gold and silver Eagles. Obverse of the gold coins is Augustus Saint-Gaudens' design used on the gold $20 coin of 1907-1933. Many consider it the most beautiful coin design in U.S. history. The gold coins' reverse, designed by Miley Busiek, shows a family of eagles with the adult returning to her young in a nest.

Obverse of the silver Eagles was adapted from Adolph Weinman's Walking Liberty design used on the half dollar of 1916-1947. It, too, is a favorite design of longtime collectors. The silver reverse features a modern but classically styled heraldic-eagle design by John Mercanti.

Design of the silver American Eagle bullion coin is based on the Walking Liberty half dollar design by Adolph Weinman (top), and design of the gold Eagle is based on the gold $20 design by Augustus Saint-Gaudens.

Where to get them

Regular strikes of silver American Eagle bullion coins can be purchased from coin and bullion dealers. The U.S. Mint does not sell them directly to the public. Instead, the Mint sells bulk quantities to distributors, who in turn wholesale the coins to retailers.

Proof versions have been produced since the coin's inception in 1986, and the current-year issue can be purchased directly from the Mint (www.usmint.gov). In 2006, the Mint began selling current-year uncirculated versions of the silver and other Eagles directly to the public.

How much?

The retail price of regular strikes of the silver American Eagle is based on the current price of silver bullion plus a small premium. Collectible uncirculated versions generally sell for $15 to $20, but prices are again subject to change depending on the current trading price for silver.

Proof silver American Eagles generally sell for $30 to $60, but some issues with lower mintages bring more. The scarcest is the 1995 proof silver Eagle with a "W" mintmark, which was included only in Eagle proof sets celebrating the series' 10th anniversary. It sells for more than $5,000, according to *Coin Prices* magazine.

Mintmarks

Regular strikes of silver American Eagle bullion coins are produced at Philadelphia and do not have a mintmark. From 1986 through 1992, proof versions were struck at San Francisco and have an "S" mintmark.

From 1993 through 2000, proof versions were struck at Philadelphia and have a "P" mintmark. In 1995, as noted, proof silver Eagles were also produced at West Point, N.Y.

These scarce coins have a "W" mintmark and were struck for inclusion in a special Eagle bullion coin proof set celebrating the program's 10th anniversary.

Since 2001, proof silver Eagles have been struck at West Point and have a "W" mintmark.

In 2006, to celebrate the silver Eagle series' 20th anniversary, the Philadelphia Mint produced a special "reverse proof" in addition to the regular West Point proof version for that year. The "reverse proof" features a frosted finish in the field and a mirror-like finish on the raised design surfaces, just the opposite (or reverse) of a traditional proof. The

1995-W proof silver Eagles were struck for special anniversary sets only.

2006 reverse proofs have a "P" mintmark and were available only in a three-coin silver Eagle set (proof, uncirculated, and reverse-proof versions).

Since 2006, as noted, the Mint has sold uncirculated versions of current-year silver Eagles directly to the public. These special collector versions are struck at West Point and have a "W" mintmark.

The mintmark on silver Eagles appears on the reverse below the eagle's right claw.

Condition

Condition is not a factor for silver Eagles bought and sold solely for their bullion content.

On collectible coins, traditional high points for wear on the Walking Liberty design are the hair on Liberty's left temple and the upper part of her left leg. Uncirculated and proof versions of the silver Eagle should be free of major scratches and other blemishes.

How to store them

Security is more of a concern than preservation for silver Eagles bought and sold solely for their bullion content. A bank safety-deposit box or other secure, fireproof system is recommended for bulk quantities of silver or other Eagle bullion coins.

For collectible versions, an inert holder in which both sides of the coin are protected is recommended. Uncirculated and proof versions should be kept in their original Mint packaging, if available.

Silver American Eagle bullion coin specs

Obverse designer: Adolph A. Weinman.

Reverse designer: John Mercanti.

Diameter: 40.6 millimeters.

Weight: 31.1010 grams.

Composition: 99.93-percent silver, 0.07-percent copper.

Actual silver weight: 0.999 troy ounces.

Silver American Eagle checklist

Uncirculated and regular strikes

_____ 1986

_____ 1987

_____ 1988

_____ 1989

_____ 1990

_____ 1991

_____ 1992

_____ 1993

_____ 1994

_____ 1995

_____ 1996

_____ 1997

_____ 1998

_____ 1999

_____ 2000

_____ 2001

_____ 2002

_____ 2003

_____ 2004

_____ 2005

_____ 2006

_____ 2006-W (uncirculated version only)

_____ 2007

_____ 2007-W (uncirculated version only)

_____ 2008

_____ 2008-W (uncirculated version only)

Series is ongoing.

The silver Eagle contains one troy ounce of 0.9993-fine silver.

Proofs

_____ 1986-S

_____ 1987-S

_____ 1988-S

_____ 1989-S

_____ 1990-S

_____ 1991-S

_____ 1992-S

_____ 1993-P

_____ 1994-P

_____ 1995-P

_____ 1995-W (Eagle 10th anniversary sets only)

_____ 1996-P

_____ 1997-P

_____ 1998-P

_____ 1999-P

_____ 2000-P

_____ 2001-W

_____ 2002-W

_____ 2003-W

_____ 2004-W

_____ 2005-W

_____ 2006-W

_____ 2006-P (reverse proof, silver Eagle 20th anniversary sets only)

_____ 2007-W

_____ 2008-W

Series is ongoing.

Since 2001, proof silver Eagles have been struck at the West Point Mint and carry a "W" mintmark on the reverse.

The fine art of fineness

Precious metal—be it gold or silver—must be alloyed with a small amount of base metal, such as copper, to make it suitable for coin production. The purity of precious metal in a coin is called "fineness," which is expressed in parts per thousand.

For example, the silver American Eagle bullion coin is 0.9993 fine, which means it has 999.3 parts of pure silver for every 1,000 parts of total metal in the coin. Thus, the coin is said to contain one troy ounce of 0.9993-fine silver.

The West Point Mint

The West Point Mint in West Point, N.Y., is not as well known as a coin-production facility as its more traditional counterparts in Philadelphia, Denver, and San Francisco. It was built in 1937 as the West Point Bullion Depository, an adjunct of the New York Assay Office.

It produced one-cent coins without a mintmark from 1973 to 1986. It was officially designated a U.S. branch mint in 1988. Its "W" mintmark first appeared on the 1986 Statue of Liberty Centennial commemorative gold $5 coin.

Chapter 14
Collecting World Coins

World coins—the hobby's common reference for coins encompassing all countries—offer a world of opportunities for collectors of all means and interests. Some historic issues dating back to the 1600s are affordable for many collectors, and like the United States, many countries today issue commemorative coins that can be purchased directly from the mint or an authorized U.S. agent.

But where do you start when the whole world of coinage is available to you?

Buy a book

Any collector needs to know what's available and how much it costs so he or she has a road map to their collecting pursuits. So start by buying a reference book on world coins.

An inexpensive book, such as "World Coins & Currency, 2nd Edition" by Arlyn G. Sieber, part of the Warman's Companion series from Krause Publications (www.krausebooks.com), can provide a good overview of world coinage.

For a complete listing of coins available from a particular country, consult the venerable and massive "Standard Catalog of World Coins," also from Krause

1902 25-cent of Canada (from top), 1964 French 5-franc of Comoros, and 1996 1-dalasi of Gambia.

Publications. The multivolume series, broken down by century, lists every coin produced in the world for the years covered. It is also now available on DVD.

A subscription to the monthly *World Coin News* (www.worldcoinnews.net) provides current information on new issues from world mints and articles on world coins of all eras.

Collecting strategies

When deciding which world coins to pursue, a collector should start with the basic guideline that applies to any coin-collecting pursuit: Collect what you like. A world coin collection can be anything an individual collector wants it to be, but following are some common collecting strategies for world coins:

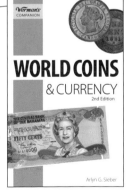

By series

The traditional coin-collecting pursuit of acquiring one example of each date and mintmark within a particular series may seem daunting at first considering the vast scope of world coins. Some series within those denominations span several decades or even a century or more.

But consulting a reference, such as the "Standard Catalog of World Coins," will reveal some shorter, affordable series that may interest an individual collector.

Books and magazines provide reference information on old and new world coins.

By country

Collectors sometimes focus on coins of a particular country because of some emotional nexus with the land. It may have been their ancestors' homeland, or they may simply like the coin designs and history of a particular country.

1711 half crown of Great Britain.

Many strategies can be pursued within the scope of collecting by country. A collector may attempt to acquire one example of each ruler whose image appeared on the country's coinage or focus on the coinage of one particular ruler. Or the collector may pursue one example of each denomination or design type produced.

1723 shilling of Great Britain.

Any of the collecting goals could also be narrowed to a certain period—a particular century, for example, or range of years with some historical or personal significance.

By region

A world-coin collection could also focus on a particular continent or geographic region within that continent. Examples of the former include coins of South America or the Middle East. Examples of the latter include coins of the German States, the Iberian Peninsula, or colonies of a particular country.

Assembling a complete collection of all coins of a particular region is

2003 10-euro of the Irish Republic.

not practical for most collectors, so a further breakdown in collecting goals is in order. That could include focusing on a particular ruler, period, denomination, or some combination thereof. It could also include some form of type collecting—one coin of each ruler, for example.

By empire

A coin collection can be a virtual history book of an empire. It would document the dates of the empire's rise to power and fall or contraction of power. It would document the rulers that reigned over the empire. And it would document the various lands that fell under the empire's domain, including the dates of conquest and the dates of loss or independence.

By era

Some collectors focus on world coins of a particular era. It could be a certain century, the reign of a certain monarch, an era with personal significance to a collector, or an important historical time.

There are many other possibilities limited only to a collector's imagination and his or her historical interests.

1937 crown of Australia.

One per country

Another common collecting strategy is to acquire one example of the coinage of as many countries as possible. Narrowing the focus here could include a particular geographic region, century, or era.

By theme

Modern commemorative and circulation coinage designs gave rise to collecting coins with a common theme. Examples include coins that depict animals or ships, coins from one or more countries that commemorate a certain event, or coins of a certain date, such as 2000.

Modern coinage can complement a collection of the classics. For example, a collection of coins from the era of exploration could be accessorized by modern coins that commemorate anniversaries associated with those explorations.

2001 500-korun of Slovakia.

A collection can also be built around a certain event. For example, Great Britain and many lands still associated with the British monarchy issued commemorative coins to mark the golden jubilee of Queen Elizabeth II's reign in 2002. These recent coins could be combined with coins from the 1950s that first depicted the queen.

By collector's choice

As noted above, various aspects of the listed strategies overlap and can be combined and mixed to form a goal that interests an individual collector. The result should be a world-coin collection that is affordable and attainable for the collector, and a collection that brings enjoyment and satisfaction.

1972 50-franc of New Caledonia.

Where to get them

A collector in the United States can't walk into his or her local bank and ask for a roll of Russian rubles they can search through, so world coins have to be purchased. They are, however, widely available at shows and shops, and through advertisements in hobby publications, such as *World Coin News*.

A bin full of inexpensive late-date world coins in 2-by-2 holders is a common site at shows and shops. Collectors can dig through the bins and look for coins that fit their collecting goals—be it a design theme or a certain country or a certain ruler.

1976 5-mark of the German Federal Republic.

Like the U.S. Mint, many world mints have Web sites through which collectors can order current-year sets and commemoratives. Reports of new issues in *World Coin News* include ordering information. Many U.S. dealers also stock current and recent world commemoratives at their shops or shows they attend.

Many world mints also display and sell their current offerings at the annual conventions and shows of the American Numismatic Association (www.money.org).

How much?

World coins cover the gamut of numismatic values. The late-date coins in bins at shows and shops can often be purchased for less than a dollar each.

Even some coins dating back to the 1600s can be purchased for less than $20 each,

1848 1-gulden of the Netherlands.

depending on the coin, its composition, and its condition. A little bit of research should reveal a world-coin collecting goal that matches any collecting budget.

Mintmarks

Just like U.S. coins, many world coins have mintmarks indicating where they were struck. References such as the "Standard Catalog of World Coins" list the mints for each country and the marks they used to designate their coinage.

2002 20-kroner of Norway.

Condition

There is no comprehensive grading guide to world coins because of the wide range of designs among the many countries. Collectors focusing on a particular world coinage type should study examples in various condition and learn to make their own assessments of high points for wear. World-coin books usually contain some general guidelines on grading. Fortunately, though, condition is not a critical factor for inexpensive world coins.

1780 8-reales of Spain.

Grading becomes more important as collectors move up in price.

How to store them

Inexpensive world coins can be left in the 2-by-2 holders in which they will

2002 100-dinars of Algeria.

probably be purchased or transferred to a folder or album. But as collectors move up in price range, appropriate care should be used when handling and storing world coins, as outlined in Chapter 1.

A wealth of mints

Mexico's first republic, established in 1823, used 14 different mints to strike coins. All the mints used the same basic designs, but many variations exist depending on the mint.

The Chinese coinage crises

China nearly ceased the striking of coins in the 1930s and '40s because of war and uncontrollable inflation. The land relied on large amounts of paper currency issued by nationalist, communist, and Japanese occupation authorities.

Coins as awards

Russian gold ducats struck prior to Peter I (1689-1725) are believed to have been awards for military personnel rather than coinage intended for circulation. The higher the rank of the person receiving the award, the bigger the coin.

Part 3

WHAT TO WATCH FOR

*Scarce coins to know
and look for in
circulation*

Chapter 15
On the Watch for "Wheat Cents"

"Wheat cents"—the common reference for Lincoln cents produced from 1909 through 1958 with the wheatears reverse—still turn up in circulation. The Lincoln-cent rolls referenced in Chapter 2 yielded one example—a 1951-D.

1911-D Lincoln wheat cent.

Wheat cents produced from 1934 through 1958 are not valuable in typical circulated condition. Still, wheat cents are easy to spot in circulation or when searching a bulk quantity of coins, and it's still possible a more scarce earlier date could turn up. So it's always worthwhile to check the date and mintmark on a wheat cent when one is found.

Also, a single example—such as the 1951-D mentioned above—can start a collection of wheat cents. Bulk quantities of wheat cents—ranging from a small plastic bag full of them to larger cloth bags containing thousands of coins—can be purchased from dealers at shops and shows or through advertisements in hobby publications such as *Coins* magazine.

1951-D Lincoln wheat cent.

A search of these bulk quantities can speed the collection of common dates in circulated grades and could possibly yield a more valuable key date.

What to watch for

The distinctive reverse for wheat cents—two stalks of wheat surrounding the words "One Cent"—easily stands out from the currently produced Lincoln cents with the Memorial reverse. Following are some key dates to watch for when happening upon a wheat cent or when searching bulk quantities of the coin.

Values listed below are approximate retail values (what you could expect to pay for the coin if you were to purchase it from a dealer) for grade VF-20. The values are based on those listed in the book "U.S. Coin Digest."

The book describes a VF-20 wheat cent as follows: "Hair, cheek, jaw, and bow-tie details will be worn but clearly separated, and wheat stalks on the reverse will be full with no weak spots."

1909-S "V.D.B.," $1,000

1909-S "V.D.B." Lincoln cent.

When the Lincoln cent was first issued in 1909, designer Victor David Brenner placed his initials at the bottom of the reverse between the stems of the two ears of wheat. Some, though, thought the initials were too prominent and pretentious, so they were removed after 1909 production had already begun. (They were resumed in 1918 but this time on the obverse and in a less-prominent style.)

The San Francisco Mint struck only 484,000 1909 Lincoln cents with its "S" mintmark on the obverse below the date and the designer's initials ("V.D.B.") on the reverse. Thus, this scarce variety is the king of Lincoln cents.

The coin must have both key elements—the "S" mintmark on the obverse and the "V.D.B." initials on the reverse—to command the value listed above. Other 1909 varieties are not as valuable.

The Philadelphia Mint also struck 1909 cents with the "V.D.B." initials on the reverse and no mintmark on the obverse, but mintage of this variety was almost 28 million. Value in VF-20 is about $8.

Later in 1909, Philadelphia struck more than 72 million 1909 Lincoln cents without the designer's initials on the reverse. Value in VF-20 is about $3.

Later in 1909, the San Francisco Mint struck more than 1.8 million Lincoln cents with its "S" mintmark but no designer initials. This variety is not as valuable as the 1909-S with the designer initials, but the 1909-S without the initials still commands about $150 in VF-20.

1914-D, $400

The Denver Mint produced fewer than 1.2 million Lincoln cents in 1914, compared to more than 75 million from the Philadelphia Mint that year. The Denver strikes have a "D" mintmark below the date on the obverse.

1914-D Lincoln cent.

1922 no mintmark, $1,700

All 1922 Lincoln cents were struck at the Denver Mint and are supposed to have a "D" mintmark. The mintmark, however, does not show up on some of the coins.

As the Denver Mint produced one-cent coins in 1922, it's believed that an obverse die and reverse die were damaged when they clashed in the coining press without a blank planchet in between. The reverse die was

1922 no-mintmark, or "plain," Lincoln cent.

replaced, but the obverse die was repaired and put back in service. In the course of the repair, however, the mintmark apparently was removed.

The above scenario was the conclusion of a 1982 study by the American Numismatic Association Certification Service.

To command the value listed earlier, "plain" 1922 cents must have no trace of the mintmark and a strong reverse strike indicative of the new reverse die. Coins struck with other die combinations—some of which show traces of the "D" mintmark—are not as valuable. Also, some 1922 cents originally struck with a "D" mintmark have been altered in an attempt to replicate the more valuable variety.

If you find a plain 1922 cent, and believe it could be the valuable variety, handle the coin carefully and place it in a 2-by 2 holder. Then show it to several dealers at a show or take it to several coin shops to get some professional opinions on its authenticity.

Also note that Lincoln wheat cents struck at the Philadelphia Mint are not supposed to have mintmarks. So Lincoln cents dated other than 1922 without mintmarks are not error coins and are not exceptionally valuable. In fact, the Philadelphia Mint struck most Lincoln wheat cents in the years it produced the coin, so the Philadelphia strikes are less valuable than the San Francisco and Denver strikes of the same year.

1931-S, $85

The San Francisco Mint struck only 866,000 Lincoln cents in 1931, compared with almost 19.4 million at the Philadelphia Mint, and 4.48 million at the Denver Mint. To get the value listed above, the coin must be dated 1931 and must have the "S" mintmark below the date.

1931-S Lincoln cent.

Lincoln wheat-cent specs

Designer: Victor David Brenner.

Size: 19 millimeters.

Weight: 3.11 grams.

Composition (1909-1942): 95-percent copper, five-percent tin and zinc.

Composition (1943): Steel coated with zinc.

Composition (1944-1958): 95-percent copper, five-percent zinc.

The steel war cents

The composition of 1943 Lincoln cents was changed from predominately copper to predominately steel to conserve on raw materials critical to the war effort. The "war cents" are easily distinguished from other Lincoln cents by their silver-gray color.

The 1943 cents are an interesting historical sidebar in the Lincoln series but command only about 50 cents retail in typical circulated grades. The Philadelphia, Denver, and San Francisco mints combined struck more than a billion of the coins.

Coin drops

You say nobody will ever find a 1909-S "V.D.B." Lincoln cent in circulation again? Indeed, chances are slim that an example of this scarce variety will slip through undetected all these years, but …

Beginning in 1990 in Seattle, and continuing for several years after in a number of other cities, representatives of the weekly *Numismatic News* spent several 1909-S "V.D.B." Lincoln cents as partial payment for such sundry items as lunch and ice cream. The "coin drops," as they came to be known, were publicity stunts for coin collecting in advance of American Numismatic Association conventions held in the respective cities in various years.

News releases announcing the drops were sent to local media, and they generated prominent newspaper and television news coverage for the hobby and upcoming convention.

None of the coins was ever reported found, so just maybe, somewhere out there …

Chapter 16
On the Watch for Doubled-die Lincoln Cents

If you see double on a Lincoln cent, you could be seeing hundreds of dollars in profit. Collectors value coins that show a distinctive doubling of their design features—like the coin is out of focus. Some are doubled-die coins that are common and worth only a few dollars each; others command higher prices.

1955 doubled-die Lincoln cent.

Following are five doubled-die Lincoln cents that have been identified by experts and are commonly listed in coin value guides. Circulating cents dated 1955, 1972, 1983, 1984, and 1995 should be checked for this doubling.

Values listed are approximate retail values (the price you could expect to pay if purchasing the coin from a dealer) and are based on the value listings in the book "U.S. Coin Digest" for examples grading XF-40.

A bin of planchets is ready to be struck into coins.

The story behind the coins

To understand doubled-die coins, one must first understand how coins are produced. Following are the three major steps in the manufacturing process:

1. Blanks are produced.

A "blank" is a round, flat piece of coin metal punched from a sheet or strip of metal. It's then given a raised edge, or rim, and it becomes a "planchet."

The planchet is the same size and composition of the coin it will become, but at this point, it is just a blank piece of metal with no design.

2. Dies are produced.

A die is a round piece of hard metal with a mirror image of the coin design engraved in recess on its face. It takes two dies to produce a coin—one with the obverse design on it and one with the reverse design on it.

Working dies—the dies from which coins are actually struck—are made by a tool called a "hub." A hub is a piece of steel with the coin design in relief on it—the same as the relief design (with the design features raised above the coin's surface) on a coin.

A blank die is softened by heating it, and then the hub is forced into the die face, which forms the incuse, mirror image of the coin design on the die face. Thousands of working dies can be made from a single hub.

3. Coins are struck.

To produce the actual coin, a blank is fed into a coining press between the obverse die and reverse die. The two dies are pressed onto the blank at tremendous pressure—about 30 tons per square inch to produce a one-cent coin—impressing the design image onto the blank. The finished coin is then ejected from the press and into a hopper.

All of this happens in a fraction of second. Modern coin presses are capable of producing hundreds of coins a minute.

How doubling occurs

To produce a working die, it must receive multiple impressions, or pressings, from the hub. Between impressions, the die is removed from the die press and softened again.

If the hub and die are not lined up properly when placed back on the die press, the subsequent pressings from the hub will not line up with the existing impression on the working die made by previous pressings. The result is a doubling of the design features on the die because the subsequent pressing is slightly offset from the previous ones.

Because the design is now doubled on the die, all coins struck from the die will show the doubling on either their obverse or reverse, depending on which die was affected by the doubling.

Because the hubbing process is the source of the doubling, this type of doubling is referred to by collectors as "hub doubling." "Most forms of hub doubling show as well-rounded, overlapping images in relief, with distinct separation lines between those images," say authors Brian Allen and Ken Potter in their book "Strike It Rich With Pocket Change" (Krause Publications, 2006).

What to watch for

1955 doubled-die Lincoln cent, $1,425

This is the king of doubled-die Lincoln cents, partly because it's the oldest and partly because the doubling is so distinct. It can be clearly seen in the date.

1955 doubled-die Lincoln cent.

The doubling occurs only on the 1955 Philadelphia strikes, which do not have a mintmark. It does not occur on the 1955 Lincoln cents with a "D" mintmark for Denver or an "S" mintmark for San Francisco.

1972 doubled-die Lincoln cent, $285

There are several known doubled-die 1972 Lincoln cents from all three mints, but the most valuable are Philadelphia strikes with distinctive doubling on the obverse. It can be seen in the date, the word "Liberty," and the motto "In God We Trust."

1972 doubled-die Lincoln cent.
Photo courtesy of Brian Allen.

1983 doubled-die Lincoln cent, $100

The doubling occurs on the reverse and is not quite as distinctive as the 1955 and 1972 cents. Check the lettering on the reverse, particularly in the words "One Cent." The doubling again occurs only on Philadelphia coins (those without mintmarks).

1983 doubled-die Lincoln cent.

The end of hub doubling?

Have we seen the last of doubled-die coins? Maybe. In the 1990s, the U.S. Mint switched to a more modern "single-squeeze" process for producing working coin dies from a hub rather than the old multiple-impression process. The new process has "virtually eliminated the possibility of hub doubling on coins in the United States starting in 1997 for the cent and five cent coins and the balance of denominations in 1998," say authors Brian Allen and Ken Potter in their book "Strike It Rich With Pocket Change."

1984 doubled-die Lincoln cent, $60

The doubling again occurs on the obverse and again is subtler than earlier doubled-die cents. Check around Lincoln's ear lobe for a doubled image. This doubling occurs only on 1984 Lincoln cents struck at Philadelphia.

1984 doubled-die Lincoln cent.

1995 doubled-die Lincoln cent, $20

The doubling occurs on the obverse and can be best seen in the letters "ber" in the word "Liberty." It can also be seen in the motto "In God We Trust." This doubling occurs only on 1995 Lincoln cents struck at Philadelphia.

1995 doubled-die Lincoln cent.

What to do if you find one

If you believe you've found one of the doubled-die Lincoln cents listed, particularly one of the more valuable dates, handle the coin carefully and place it in a 2-by-2 holder. Then show it to several dealers at a show or take it to several coin shops to get some professional opinions on its authenticity.

Doubled with two d's

Some sources refer to "double-die" coins, but the term is more precisely written as "doubled-die" because the design on the working die is doubled, creating the doubled image on the coin. The doubled image did not occur because "double dies" were used.

Chapter 17
On the Watch for
1950-D Jefferson Nickels

In the 1950s and '60s, the 1950-D Jefferson nickel was one of the hottest things on the market. Demand for this otherwise unassuming coin has cooled in recent years, but it's still well worth putting aside if you happen upon one when searching rolls of Jefferson nickels.

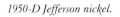

1950-D Jefferson nickel.

The story behind the coin

Coin collecting was entering a boom period in the early 1950s. War veterans came home and started earning a living wage, which allowed them to pursue hobbies like coin collecting. Older collectible coins, such as Indian cents and Liberty nickels, could still be found in circulation.

There were more publications on coin collecting, so there was more information on the hobby. Collectors became more aware of hobby news like mintage figures for current or late-date coinage.

Thus, when it became known in the early 1950s that the Denver Mint produced "only" 2.63 million five-cent coins in 1950, the rush was on for 1950-D Jefferson nickels. In contrast, the Philadelphia Mint produced more than 9.8 million nickels that year.

In 1949, Philadelphia produced more than 60 million nickels, Denver produced more than 36 million, and San Francisco produced more than 9.7 million. In 1951, Philadelphia produced more than 28 million nickels, Denver produced more than 20 million, and San Francisco produced more than 7.7 million.

Although a couple of million coins is still a couple of million coins, the 1950-D mintage was significantly lower than other Jefferson nickel date and mintmark combinations of the era. In 1957, Denver produced more than 168 million Jefferson nickels.

Collectors of the 1950s began hoarding every 1950-D Jefferson nickel they could get their hands on. By 1964, when the Philadelphia and Denver mints combined produced more than 2.8 billion Jefferson nickels, the 1950-D's mintage seemed even more paltry.

The mintmark is located on the reverse on 1950 Jefferson nickels.

Still, though, a couple of million coins is a couple of million coins. With collectors putting aside every '50-D nickel they could find, it became apparent later in the 1960s and '70s that plenty of collectible examples existed to meet market demand.

Values for 1950-D nickels have stabilized since the late 1950s and early '60s, but they still have the lowest mintage in the Jefferson series. With nickel mintages today in the hundreds of millions, it's unlikely the U.S. Mint will ever produce a circulating Jefferson nickel with a lower mintage.

What to watch for

They're easy to spot. Look for the 1950 date on the obverse and the "D" mintmark on the reverse to the right of Monticello.

How much?

Retail values for 1950-D Jefferson nickels in typical circulated grades range from $10 to $15. Even well-worn examples reach the lower level of that price range.

What to do if you find one

Follow the rules in Chapter 1 for safe handling of coins and place the coin in a 2-by-2 holder or another type of safe storage system in which both sides of the coin are protected.

The Denver Mint

An 1862 congressional act established a U.S. assay office in Denver, but full-fledged branch-mint status came later. Coin production began in 1906. Denver continues to produce all denominations of currently circulating coins.

In U.S. coinage history, Denver shares its "D" mintmark with the Dahlonega (Georgia) Mint, which struck gold coins in various years from 1838 through 1861.

Chapter 18
On the Watch for
1982 No-mintmark Dimes

Oops! That may have been the collective reaction of U.S. Mint officials and workers when they discovered an important design element was left off a Philadelphia Mint working die for 1982 dimes—namely, the "P" mintmark.

In the years since its discovery, the 1982 no-mintmark dime has become one of the classic error coins of all time. It's believed the number struck was small, but it's still a candidate to turn up in circulation for those who know of its existence and what to look for.

1982 no-mintmark dime.

The story behind the coin

The Roosevelt dime was introduced in 1946 as a tribute to the late President Franklin D. Roosevelt. Calls for Roosevelt to be honored on a coin came soon after his death on April 12, 1945.

Congressional approval is required to change any coin design that has been used for less than 25 years. At the time of Roosevelt's death, the Lincoln cent (introduced in 1909), the so-called Mercury dime (1916), and the Walking Liberty half dollar (1916) were eligible for redesign.

The Roosevelt dime replaced the Mercury dime (pictured) in 1946.

The dime was chosen for Roosevelt because the March of Dimes was a fund-raising campaign for the National Foundation for Infantile Paralysis, which Roosevelt established in 1938. Roosevelt suffered from the disease, commonly called polio. Mint engraver John R. Sinnock designed the coin.

The Philadelphia, Denver, and San Francisco mints produced circulation strikes of the Roosevelt dime from 1946 through 1955. Denver and Philadelphia have continued to produce Roosevelt dimes for circulation since 1956. San Francisco has produced proof versions since 1968.

From 1946 through 1964, Roosevelt dimes produced at Philadelphia did not have a mintmark. Those produced at

Denver had a "D" mintmark, and those produced at San Francisco had an "S" mintmark.

From 1965 through 1967, no U.S. coins had mintmarks.

From 1968 through 1979, Roosevelt dimes produced at Philadelphia did not have a mintmark, but those produced at Denver resumed the "D" mintmark and the proof versions produced at San Francisco carried an "S" mintmark.

Beginning in 1980, the "P" mintmark was added to Roosevelt dimes produced at Philadelphia. Maybe the Philadelphia Mint workers were too used to producing coins without a mintmark for so many years. Whatever the reason, a working die without a "P" mintmark added to it was put into production at Philadelphia and apparently went unnoticed for a significant period.

Philadelphia-produced Roosevelt dimes did not have mintmarks from 1968 through 1979.

The error became known to the coin-collecting community in early 1983 when 1982 dimes without mintmarks started showing up in Ohio. The discovery was front-page news in *Numismatic News* for weeks.

Detail of the mintmark area on the 1982 no-mintmark dime.

What to watch for

The error appears on Roosevelt dimes dated 1982 only. The mintmark is supposed to appear on the obverse just above the date. This area should show absolutely no trace of a mintmark.

The usual mintmark location on Roosevelt dimes is above the date on the obverse.

A faint outline of a mintmark in this area may indicate simply a weak strike, possibly caused by dirt or grease filling in the mintmark area on the working die, or a weak attempt at altering a 1982 dime with a mintmark.

How much?

A 1982 no-mintmark dime is worth about $25 to $50 in typical circulated grades.

Why no mintmarks in 1965-1967?

Mintmarks were eliminated from U.S. coins dated 1965-1967 in an effort to streamline production. It was one of several steps the U.S. Mint took at the time in response to a coin shortage.

See Chapter 20 for more on the coin shortage of the early to mid-1960s.

What to do if you find one

If you believe you've found a 1982 no-mintmark dime, follow the rules in Chapter 1 for safe handling of coins and place it in a 2-by-2 holder. Then show it to several dealers at a show or take it to several coin shops to get some professional opinions on its authenticity.

It's only the '82 that's valuable

"Hey, I found a 1978 dime without a mintmark. How much is it worth?"

Answer: 10 cents.

As noted, Roosevelt dimes produced at Philadelphia before 1980 are not supposed to have mintmarks. Therefore, pre-1980 Roosevelt dimes produced for circulation without mintmarks are not errors and are not scarce.

It is only the 1982-dated dime without a mintmark that is in error.

The March of Dimes today

The National Foundation for Infantile Paralysis officially changed its name to the March of Dimes in 1979. Today, its work focuses on supporting polio survivors and researching birth defects in general.

Chapter 19
On the Watch for the "Extra-leaf" Wisconsin Quarter

It's one of those things that only a sharp-eyed coin collector would notice, but it set the coin-collecting community on its collective ear, so to speak, when it was discovered.

In early 2005, a number of 2004 Wisconsin quarters, part of the U.S. Mint's 50 State Quarters Program, were discovered with what appears to be an "extra leaf" in the ear of corn on the reverse. The coin community, and even the general media—including CNN, *USA Today*, and National Public Radio—were abuzz with the news, and values for the variety shot up.

2004-D Wisconsin quarter, as it was intended to appear.

Values have since settled in, but the two varieties of "extra-leaf" Wisconsin quarters are still some of the most significant coins that can conceivably be found in circulation.

The story behind the coin

The Wisconsin quarter was released Oct. 25, 2004, with the usual amount of fanfare accompanying the release of each coin in the 50 State Quarters Program within each respective state. The reverse features simplistic depictions of a cow, an ear of corn, and a wheel of cheese—certainly symbolic of one major industry in the state but falling short on artistic merit.

In early 2005, however, the coin started making national news when collectors in the Southwest noticed the ear of corn appeared to have an "extra leaf" on some coins produced at the Denver Mint ("D" mintmark). When the news broke, the scramble was on to find the coins with the unintentional variety, and speculation as to what caused it was rampant.

The "extra leaf" appears to the viewer's left of the ear of corn beneath the large turned-down leaf. As the coins surfaced, two varieties were detected: One has the "extra leaf" pointed downward (listed as "leaf low" in some value guides), and the second has the "extra leaf" pointed upward ("leaf high").

About a year after the coins were discovered, the mystery as to what caused the variety was solved when *USA Today* obtained a copy of the Mint's official report on the incident through the Freedom of Information Act. In its Jan. 20, 2006, issue, the newspaper reported that an ill-timed meal break by a Denver Mint worker was the cause.

The report said a press operator at the branch mint noticed blemishes on the Wisconsin quarters being produced on one of the five machines he was operating. He stopped the machine, but then left for a meal break before correcting the problem.

When he returned to work, the machine was running again, so he assumed that another worker had changed the working die being used to strike the quarters. About an hour and a half later, it was discovered the problem had not been resolved and that thousands of coins with the "extra leaf" had been struck and comingled with regular coins produced by the other presses.

By the time the mistake was discovered, according to the *USA Today* report, the coins were already bagged and ready for shipment. The newspaper reported that as many as 50,000 entered circulation. The book "U.S. Coin Digest" estimates the total mintage at 12,000.

What to watch for

The variety appears on 2004 Wisconsin quarters struck at the Denver Mint only ("D" mintmark on the obverse below the words "In God We Trust"). Check the area to the left of the ear of corn, below the large turned-down leaf on the reverse, for another smaller leaf emanating from the ear.

A normal Wisconsin quarter (top), the "leaf low" variety (middle), and the "leaf high" variety (bottom).
Photos courtesy of Ken Potter.

On some coins with the variety, the "extra leaf" is turned down in an arc toward the wheel of cheese ("leaf low"). On others, it points upward toward the larger leaf above it ("leaf high").

How much?

The "leaf high" variety is the scarcer of the two, according to "U.S. Coin Digest." The book estimates its mintage at 3,000. Mintage for the "leaf low" variety is estimated at 9,000.

Three-coin sets (one regular example and the two varieties) in high-uncirculated grades have sold for thousands of dollars. Expect much less for one found in circulation with typical wear—around $50. The scarcer "leaf high" variety will garner a bit more.

What to do if you find one

Follow the rules in Chapter 1 for safe handling of coins and place the coin in a 2-by-2 holder or another type of safe storage system in which both sides of the coin are protected. Then show it to several dealers at a show or take it to several coin shops to get some professional opinions on its authenticity. As always, scarce varieties are susceptible to nefarious attempts at replication by altering a common coin.

Cheese whiz! That's a lot of ideas

According to the U.S. Mint's official profile of the Wisconsin state quarter, the state's governor received more than 9,600 design suggestions for the coin. That's more than half the number of dairy farms in the state (17,000) and almost 30 times the number of variety of cheeses produced in the state (more than 350).

Chapter 20
On the Watch for Silver Coins

Until 1965, U.S. dimes, quarters, and half dollars were struck in the traditional composition of 90-percent silver and 10-percent copper. In early 2008, silver bullion traded at $15 to $20 a troy ounce. That made the silver in a pre-1965 quarter worth $2.71 to $3.61.

Although most of the old silver coinage has been culled from circulation over the years, silver coins of current design (Roosevelt dime, Washington quarter, and Kennedy half dollar) still slip through now and then.

The last of the 90-percent-silver dimes (pictured), quarters, and half dollars were dated 1964.

The story behind the coins

Until 1961, the U.S. government controlled the price of silver in the country, setting it at 92.5 cents an ounce. But after 1961, silver bullion was allowed to trade on the free market and government controls on its price were lifted. Silver soon shot up to $1.29 an ounce.

By 1964, it cost the government more than 25 cents to produce a quarter because of the increase in silver prices. The high cost of silver coupled with increasing demand for coinage, in part from the growing popularity of vending machines, led to a coin shortage in the country.

In response, President Lyndon Johnson signed into law the Coinage Act of 1965, which eliminated silver from the dime and quarter, and replaced it with a clad composition consisting largely of copper. The half dollar was reduced to

40-percent silver (see Chapter 21).

The act also suspended the production of proof and mint sets for sale to collectors so the U.S. Mint could concentrate on circulating-coin production. It also eliminated mintmarks on coins in another effort to streamline production.

Any silver coins still produced in 1965 were to be dated 1964; the new clad coins were to be dated 1965 until the shortage was resolved, even if that was into 1966 or beyond.

The clad coins continue to be struck today, and are fixtures of U.S. circulating coinage. As the clad coins entered circulation, the public hoarded the old silver coins, which were worth more than face value because of their precious-metal content and the rising price of silver.

What to watch for

The silver dimes, quarters, and half dollars are easy to distinguish: Any example dated 1964 or earlier has a composition consisting of 90-percent silver. In addition, it's always a good idea to check found coins for key dates—those with lower mintages that command a numismatic premium over their bullion value. To determine key dates, consult a current value guide, such as *Coin Prices* magazine, available on many newsstands.

A simple date check is all that's required to distinguish a silver quarter (top) from a clad quarter (bottom).

How much?

The silver value chart on page 178 shows the bullion value of silver dimes, quarters, and half dollars at various silver prices. Many Web sites report current silver prices, including the financial sections of daily newspapers.

What to do if you find one

No special precautions need to be taken with silver coins found in circulation if they display the typical amount of wear one can expect to find on them. For a coin in better condition or a key date, follow the rules in Chapter 1 for safe handling of coins and place it in a 2-by-2 holder or another storage system in which both sides of the coin are protected.

Silver quarters contain 0.1809 troy ounces of precious metal.

If you want to sell the coin, it's unlikely a dealer will want to mess around with purchasing just one silver dime or quarter unless it is a key date. The dealer may, however, be interested in purchasing a larger quantity of silver coins for their bullion value.

Consider keeping any silver coins found and using them as a start to a complete collection of Roosevelt dimes, Washington quarters, or Kennedy half dollars.

Key quarter dates

Washington quarters with "D" and "S" mintmarks dated from the series inception in 1932 through 1940 command numismatic premiums above their bullion value. The 1932-D and 1932-S are the two key dates and command significant premiums—about $200 each in typical circulated grades.

There are also two over-engraved mintmarks to watch for: the 1950 "D" over "S" and the 1950 "S" over "D." In these two instances, the dominant mintmark was engraved over the underlying mintmark on the working die. On the resulting coins, a faint outline of the underlying mintmark can be seen under the dominant mintmark.

Each variety is worth about $50 in typical circulated grades. The mintmark for these dates appears on the reverse above the "R" in the word "Quarter."

How much silver?

Following are actual silver weights for pre-1965 dimes, quarters, and half dollars:

Dime: 0.0724 troy ounces.

Quarter: 0.1809 troy ounces.

Half dollar: 0.3618 troy ounces.

Silver value chart

The following chart shows the precious-metal value of silver dimes, quarters, and half dollars at various prices per troy ounce for silver bullion.

	$10	**12.50**	**15**	**17.50**	**20**	**22.50**	**25**
Dime	$0.72	0.90	1.08	1.26	1.44	1.63	1.81
Quarter	$1.81	2.26	2.71	3.16	3.61	4.07	4.52
Half dollar	$3.61	4.52	5.42	6.33	7.23	8.14	9.04

War nickels

When searching Jefferson nickels, collectors should watch for examples dated 1942 through 1945. These wartime nickels were struck from 56-percent copper, 35-percent silver, and nine-percent manganese. They contain 0.0563 troy ounces of silver.

If the date isn't enough to distinguish them, look for the big mintmark ("P," "D," or "S") above the dome of Monticello on the reverse. For nickels struck during the war years, the mintmark was moved from its usual location to the right of Jefferson's home.

Chapter 21
On the Watch for 1965-1970 Kennedy Half Dollars

Kennedy half dollars dated 1965 through 1970 were also the targets of hoarders in the 1960s and '70s. The reason was the 0.148 troy ounces of precious metal in each of the 40-percent-silver coins.

Many were culled from pocket change and sources of bulk change during this time, but others may still be hiding in circulation thanks to the continued use of the Kennedy design for the half dollar and a lack of knowledge among the general public about the coin's precious-metal content.

1967 Kennedy half dollar.

The story behind the coin

The U.S. dime, quarter, and half dollar were still struck in the 90-percent-silver composition when the Kennedy half dollar was put on the fast track to production in late 1963 and early 1964 (see Chapter 7). So the Kennedy half saw one year (1964) of production in the traditional composition.

The Coinage Act of 1965, however, which converted the dime and quarter to a base-metal clad composition, changed the half dollar's composition to 80-percent silver and 20-percent copper bonded to a core of 20.9-percent silver and 79.1-percent copper. The net result was the 40-percent-silver composition and the 0.148 troy ounces of precious metal.

As the only precious-metal U.S. coins still in production, many 1965-1970 Kennedy half dollars were squirreled away by the public instead of remaining in circulation, even though silver prices at the time kept the half's bullion value below its 50-cent face value. The U.S. Mint couldn't produce enough of them to meet demand. It produced more than 295 million 1967 Kennedy half dollars for circulation. The following year, the Denver Mint (the only mint to produce half dollars for circulation in 1968) produced more than 246 million. The large mintages were also cutting into the government's silver reserves.

Congress responded in 1970 by passing a law changing the Kennedy half dollar's composition to the same clad composition used in the dime and quarter starting with 1965-dated coins (75-percent copper and 25-percent nickel bonded to a pure copper core). The clad composition for the half dollar was first used on 1971-dated coins and continues today.

The switch to a base-metal composition and increasing silver prices accelerated the culling of 1965-1970 Kennedy half dollars from circulation in the 1970s. In 1974, the average daily price of silver was $4.71, making the bullion content of a 40-percent-silver half dollar worth 70 cents.

What to watch for

A simple date check—1965 through 1970—is all that's required to detect a 40-percent-silver Kennedy half dollar. Circulation strikes without mintmarks were produced from 1965 through 1967. Collector versions for inclusion in Special Mint Sets (see Chapter 12) were also struck in these years.

From 1968 through 1970, only the Denver Mint produced Kennedy half dollars for circulation. They carry a "D" mintmark on the obverse below Kennedy's neckline.

The San Francisco Mint produced only proof examples in 1968, 1969, and 1970. These special versions were sold directly to collectors and have an "S" mintmark.

What to do if you find one

No special precautions need to be taken with 40-percent-silver Kennedy half dollars found in circulation if they display the typical amount of wear one can expect to find on them. For a coin in better condition, particularly the 1970-D (see sidebar), follow the rules in Chapter 1 for safe handling of coins and place it in a 2-by-2 holder or another storage system in which both sides of the coin are protected.

If you want to sell the coin, it's unlikely a dealer will want to bother with purchasing just one silver Kennedy half dollar. The dealer may, however, be interested in purchasing a larger quantity of silver coins for their bullion value.

Consider keeping any 40-percent-silver half dollars found in circulation and putting them toward a complete collection of Kennedy half dollars from 1964 to date.

Key date: 1970-D

The U.S. Mint produced only 2.15 million 1970 Kennedy half dollars for circulation, all with a "D" mintmark for Denver. According to the book "U.S. Coin Digest," a 1970-D Kennedy half dollar sells for about $38 in the uncirculated grade of MS-65.

Prices for a coin in typical circulated grades will be substantially lower, but a 1970-D Kennedy half dollar found in circulation may still be worth a little extra care in its handling and storage.

40-percent-silver Kennedy half dollar checklist

_____ 1965
_____ 1965 Special Mint Set version
_____ 1966
_____ 1966 Special Mint Set version
_____ 1967
_____ 1967 Special Mint Set version
_____ 1968-D
_____ 1968-S (proofs only)
_____ 1969-D
_____ 1969-S (proofs only)
_____ 1970-D
_____ 1970-S (proofs only)

Above: 1968-1970 proof Kennedy half dollars have an "S" mintmark. Below: Special Mint Sets were produced in 1965, 1966, and 1967.

Silver value chart

The following chart shows the precious-metal value of 40-percent-silver Kennedy half dollars at various prices per troy ounce for silver bullion. Silver prices are on the top row; the corresponding coin bullion value is on the bottom row.

$10	12.50	15	17.50	20	22.50	25
$1.48	1.85	2.22	2.59	2.96	3.33	3.70

Part 4

SPEAKING OF COINS

Numismatic terms to know and an introduction to grading

Chapter 22
The Language of Coins

Like any field, coin collecting has its own jargon and lingo. A study of the following terms will have you talking like a numismatist in no time.

Alloy

A metal or mixture of metals added to the primary metal in the coinage composition, often as a means of facilitating hardness during striking. For example, most U.S. silver and gold coins contain an alloy of 90-percent precious metal and 10-percent copper.

1887-O (New Orleans Mint) Morgan silver dollar.

Authentication

The act of determining whether a coin, medal, token, or other related item is a genuine product of the issuing authority. A recognized expert in the field, either an individual or a professional grading service, usually does the authenticating.

Bag marks

Scrapes and impairments to a coin's surface obtained after minting by contact with other coins. The term originates from the storage of coins in bags, but such marks can occur as coins leave the presses and enter hoppers in bulk. A larger coin is more susceptible to marks, which affect its grade and, therefore, its value.

Base metal

A metal with low intrinsic value. The clad coins struck for circulation in the United States today are considered base-metal coins because they are composed of copper and nickel rather than precious metals such as gold, silver, or platinum.

Coin alignment

Take a coin out of your pocket and hold it between your thumb and forefinger with the obverse ("heads" side) facing you. Using the forefinger on your other hand, spin it around so the reverse ("tails" side) faces you. The reverse will be upside down. This alignment of obverse and reverse is called "coin alignment" because it has traditionally been used on coins. In contrast, see the entries for "medal" and "medal alignment."

An illustration of coin alignment.

Commemorative

An official, government-issued coin to honor a special event or person. Commemoratives are usually sold directly to collectors at a premium above face value by the issuing authority, such as the U.S. Mint.

Counterfeit

A coin, medal, or other numismatic item made fraudulently either for entry into circulation or sale to collectors. Among the general public, counterfeiting is usually associated with paper money that is illicitly produced and spent. In numismatics, counterfeiting can involve outright attempts to produce a rare coin from scratch. It can also involve altering a common coin to make it look like a scarce variety. For instance, a counterfeiter may try to remove the mintmark from a 1982 Roosevelt dime to try to pass it off as one of the scarce 1982 no-mintmark dimes (see Chapter 18).

Die

A cylindrical piece of metal containing an incuse image of a coin design that imparts a raised image when stamped into a planchet on a coining press.

Commemoratives from Guernsey (top) and Barbados mark Queen Elizabeth II's 70th birthday.

Double eagle

An official name, as designated by law, for the U.S. gold $20 coin struck for circulation from 1849 through 1932.

A gold $20 coin, or double eagle.

Eagle

An official name, as designated by law, for the U.S. gold $10 coin struck for circulation from 1795 through 1933.

A gold $10 coin, or eagle.

Edge

The cylindrical surface of a coin between the two sides. The edge can be plain, reeded, ornamented, or lettered.

Presidential $1 coins have lettered edges.

Face value

The nominal, legal-tender value assigned to a given coin by the governing authority.

Grading

The largely subjective practice of providing a numerical or adjectival ranking of a coin's condition. See Chapter 23 for more on grading.

Half eagle

An official name, as designated by law, for the U.S. gold $5 coin struck for circulation from 1795 through 1929.

Hub

A piece of die steel showing the coinage devices in relief, or raised, as they are on a coin. The hub is pressed into the blank die, resulting in an incused, mirror image on the die. The die is then pressed into a planchet, or coin blank, on a coining press, to produce a coin.

A gold $5 coin, or half eagle.

Lettered edge

Incused or raised lettering on a coin's edge.

Medal

A coin-like object produced to commemorate an event or person. Unlike a coin, a medal is not legal tender and has no value imprinted on it. It is usually larger (two inches in diameter, for example) and thicker than a coin. Governments sometimes issue and sell medals. For example, the U.S. Mint produces and sells medals to commemorate the inauguration of a new president. Private organizations and individuals can also issue medals.

Medal alignment

Medals are generally struck with the coinage dies facing the same direction during striking. If you were to conduct the same exercise described under "coin alignment" with a medal, the reverse would be right side up instead of upside down.

Mintage

The total number of coins struck during a given time frame, generally one year. Coin listings in value guides, such as *Coin Prices* magazine, usually include mintages.

Mintmark

A letter or other marking on a coin's surface to identify the mint at which the coin was struck. Mintmarks currently used on U.S. coins are a "P" for the Philadelphia Mint, "D" for Denver, "S" for San Francisco, and "W" for West Point.

Numismatics, numismatist

Numismatics (pronounced "new-miss-MAT-iks") is the science, study, or collecting of coins, tokens, medals, paper money, and related items. One who participates in this science is a numismatist (pronounced "new-MISS-mat-ist").

Planchet

A blank disc of metal on which the image of the dies are impressed in a coining press, resulting in a finished coin. Also sometimes called a "blank."

An illustration of medal alignment.

Proof

A type of coin produced specially for sale to collectors. It is produced from specially polished dies and planchets, and receives more than one striking in the coining press. Modern silver proofs often have what are called "frosted" surfaces, which is a white finish on the raised design devices, such as a bust on the obverse.

Note the "frosted," or white design surfaces, on this proof 50 States Quarter.

Quarter eagle

A gold $2.50 coin, or quarter eagle.

An official name, as designated by law, for the U.S. gold $2.50 coin struck for circulation from 1796 through 1929.

Reeding

The serrated (tooth-like) ornamentation applied to a coin's edge during striking. U.S. dimes, quarters, and half dollars currently produced for circulation have reeded edges. The one-cent and five-cent coins have plain edges.

Series

The complete group of coins of the same denomination and design, and representing all issuing mints. For example, the Roosevelt dime series has been struck since 1946. The 50 State Quarters program is another example of a coin series.

Slabs

A nickname for coins graded by a professional coin-grading service and then sealed in a plastic holder with the coin's description, the grade assigned by the service, and a unique serial number. See Chapter 23 for more on grading and grading services.

A "slab" from the Numismatic Guaranty Corp. grading service.

Token

A privately issued piece, generally in round metal, with a represented value in trade or for a service. Businesses in the 1800s and early 1900s used tokens as promotional items and, in some cases, as substitutes for change during coinage shortages. The tokens carried inscriptions such as "Good for 10 Cents at Bob's Grocery." In more recent years, casinos have issued tokens. The tokens are sold to patrons, who use them instead of cash when gambling.

Merchant tokens were common in the 1800s and early 1900s.

Type coin

A coin that is collected because it represents a basic design of a particular denomination. For example, a type set of 20th-century U.S. quarters would consist of one example each of the Barber type (1892-1916), the Standing Liberty type (1916-1930), and the Washington type (1932 to present). Many collectors turn to type collecting because it is easier and provides more financial flexibility than trying to assemble an example of each date and mintmark combination of an entire series. In the quarter type-set example above, type collectors can choose any date and mintmark combination from any of the dates listed for each type. The collecting goal is an example of each design type rather than specific date and mintmark combinations.

Parts of a coin

Exergue

The lower segment of a coin, below the main design, generally separated by a line and often containing the date, designer initials, and mintmark.

Obverse

The front, or "heads," side of a coin.

Relief

Describes the portion of a design raised above the coin's surface, such as the bust of Washington on the quarter. The highest points of a coin's relief are most susceptible to wear in circulation and are the key areas to check when grading a coin.

Field

The flat area of a coin's obverse or reverse, devoid of design devices or inscriptions.

Variety

Any coin with a design feature different from the usual design for a particular coin series. The 1982 no-mintmark dime (see Chapter 18), for example, is a variety of the Roosevelt dime. The "extra-leaf" Wisconsin quarters (see Chapter 19) are varieties of that series.

Legend

The coin's principal lettering, generally shown along its outer perimeter. "United States of America" is an example of a legend on U.S. coins.

Obverse of a Standing Liberty quarter.

Reverse

The back, or "tails" side, of a coin.

Rim

The raised area of a coin bordering the edge and surrounding the field.

Reverse of a Standing Liberty quarter.

Chapter 23
An Introduction to Grading

Classified ads for used cars often contain some indication of the vehicle's condition. "Good condition." "Clean car." "No rust." "Low mileage." "Good runner."

The condition designations are informal and open to interpretation. Ultimately, a potential buyer must look at the car, assess its condition firsthand, and determine whether he or she wants to make a viable offer for it. If the buyer and seller can't get together on a price or the buyer determines the car just isn't right for him or her, then the buyer should thank the seller for his or her time and keep looking.

Coin grading—the process of assigning designated terms to concisely describe a coin's condition—has a more formal and defined structure than the informal language often used in selling used cars. Still, it is not an exact process. Two longtime collectors can legitimately disagree on a coin's grade, especially among uncirculated coins.

1882 Indian cent (top) and 1907 Liberty nickel. 1925-D Mercury dime (lower left).

Like buying a used car, a coin buyer must look at the coin, assess its condition firsthand, and determine whether he or she wants to make a viable offer for it. If the buyer or seller can't get together on a price or the buyer determines the coin just isn't right for them, then the buyer should thank the seller for his or her time and keep looking.

Hobby legend says that a collector walked up to a crusty old dealer at a show one time and asked the dealer to grade a coin the collector brought with him. The dealer looked at the coin and said, "I grade it a hundred dollars."

Such is the bottom line to grading coins. Ultimately, it comes down to whether the buyer likes the coin and how much he or she is willing to pay for it.

A little background

Since the early days of coin collecting, buying through the mail has been a convenient way for collectors to acquire coins. As a result, there has always been a need in numismatics for a concise way to classify the amount of wear on a coin and its condition in general.

In September 1888, Dr. George Heath, a physician in Monroe, Mich., published a four-page pamphlet titled *The American Numismatist*. Publication of subsequent issues led to the founding of the American Numismatic Association, and *The Numismatist*, as it's known today, is the association's official journal. Heath's first issues were largely devoted to selling world coins from his collection. There were no formal grades listed with the coins and their prices, but the following statement by Heath indicates that condition was a consideration for early collectors:

"The coins are in above average condition," Heath wrote, "and so confident am I that they will give satisfaction, that I agree to refund the money in any unsatisfactory sales on the return of the coins."

As coin collecting became more popular, grading became more formal. "Poor," "fair," "good," "fine," and "uncirculated" became common terms for grading coins. But modifiers, such as "about good," "very good," "extremely fine," and "about uncirculated," were soon added to these basic terms to describe coins that fell in between the major classifications. The modified terms indicated a desire for more precision in grading coins, but also reflected the process' subjective nature.

1815 Capped Bust quarter.

Books on coin grading started to appear in the late 1950s. They described and illustrated each coin grading term as they applied to each coin type. The books brought more universal definition to grading, though the process will forever maintain a certain degree of subjectivity.

The most common grading terminology used today is a combination of adjectives and numbers, as described below. The numbers range from 1 to 70, with mint state, or uncirculated, grades beginning at 60.

Grading circulated coins

Following are commonly used terms and descriptions for grading circulated coins (those with wear on them) from best to worst. The complete term—adjective and number—is given first; the commonly used shorthand version follows in parenthesis. Sometimes just the shorthand letters are used without the accompanying number. Silver dollars are used to illustrate each term.

About uncirculated-50 (AU-50)

Just a slight trace of wear, the result of brief exposure to circulation or light rubbing from mishandling, may be evident on the highest design areas. These imperfections may appear as scratches or dull spots, along with bag marks or edge nicks. At least half of the original mint luster generally is still evident.

AU-50.

Extremely fine-40 (EF-40 or XF-40)

Only slight evidence of wear is present on the design's highest points, particularly in hair lines on the obverse portrait. A trace of mint luster may still show in protected areas of the coin's surface.

Very fine-20 (VF-20)

Light wear can be seen on the fine points in the design, though it may remain sharp overall. Although the details may be slightly smooth, all lettering and major features must remain sharp.

EF-40.

Fine-12 (F-12)

Wear is moderate to considerable but generally even on all high points of the design. All elements of the design and lettering remain bold. On 20th century and later coins, the rim must be fully raised and sharp.

F-12.

VG-8.

Very good-8 (VG-8)

The coin will show considerable wear, with most detail points worn nearly smooth. On 20th century and later coins, the rim will start to merge with the lettering.

Good-4 (G-4)

Only the basic design remains distinguishable in outline form. All detail points are worn smooth. The rims are almost merging with the lettering.

G-4.

Grading uncirculated coins

The subjectivity of grading and the trend toward more classifications becomes more acute when venturing into uncirculated, or mint-state, coins. A minute difference of one or two grade points can mean a difference in value of hundreds or even thousands of dollars. In addition, the standards are more difficult to articulate in writing and illustrate through drawings or photographs. Thus, the possibilities for differences of opinion on one or two grade points increase in uncirculated coins.

MS-65 (top) and MS-63 Morgan silver dollars.

Back in Dr. George Heath's day, and continuing through the 1960s, a coin was either uncirculated or it wasn't. Little distinction was made between uncirculated coins of varying condition, largely because there was little if any difference in value.

But as collectible coins increased in value and buyers of uncirculated coins became pickier, distinctions within uncirculated grades started to surface. By the 1970s, two terms were used to grade uncirculated coins: (1) mint-state-60 (MS-60), which was a "typical uncirculated" coin, and (2) mint-state-65 (MS-65), which was a "choice uncirculated" coin. By the 1980s, four grades of uncirculated—the two listed plus MS-63 and MS-67—were used for popular upper-end coins, such as silver dollars.

Then in 1986, a new entity appeared that has changed the nature of grading and trading uncirculated coins ever since. A group of dealers led by David Hall of Newport Beach, Calif., formed the Professional Coin Grading Service. For a fee, collectors can submit a coin through an authorized PCGS dealer and receive back a professional opinion of its grade.

The Professional Coin Grading Service brought many changes to the grading and trading of high-end uncirculated coins.

After grading, the coin is encapsulated in an inert, hard-plastic holder with a serial number and the service's opinion on its grade indicated on the holder. The holders quickly earned the nickname "slabs."

In one of its most far-reaching moves, PCGS said it would use all 11 increments of uncirculated on the 70-point numerical scale: MS-60-MS-70. Several other commercial grading services followed in the steps of PCGS, and third-party grading is now an accepted part of the hobby.

Proof coins receive their own grading designation.

How should a collector approach the buying and grading of uncirculated coins? Collecting uncirculated coins worth thousands of dollars implies a higher level of numismatic expertise by the buyer. Those buyers without that level of expertise should cut their teeth on more inexpensive coins, as outlined in this book, just as today's experienced collectors did.

Grading proof coins

Because proof coins are struck by a special process, they receive their own grading designation. A coin does not start out being a proof and then become mint state if it becomes worn. Once a proof coin, always a proof coin.

In grading proof coins, the term proof always precedes the numerical designation, such as proof-65, proof-55, and proof-45.

Books on grading illustrate each coin type in each grade.

How to learn more about grading

Books

The two most widely used grading books are "The Official American Numismatic Association Grading Standards for United States Coins" (Whitman Publishing), edited by Kenneth Bressett, and "Photograde" (Zyrus Press Publishing) by James F. Ruddy. Both books illustrate and describe each specific U.S. coin type in each grade.

Both books are widely available at coin shops and shows, from the American Numismatic Association (www.money. org), larger bookstores, online booksellers, or possibly through special order at local bookstores.

American Numismatic Association

The ANA offers grading seminars at its two annual conventions, various other conventions hosted by state and regional organizations, and at its Summer Seminar series, held annually at the association's headquarters in Colorado Springs, Colo. The ANA also offers correspondence courses on grading.

All of these 1964 Jefferson nickels were found in rolls. Arranging coins of the same date and type in varying condition from worst to best can help new collectors learn how to grade.

Experience

Book knowledge and seminar knowledge can form an excellent basis for learning how to grade coins, but there's no substitute for simply looking at a lot of coins and learning to make judgments on condition and its relationship to value for yourself.

The searches of coin rolls described in various chapters in this book are a good starting point. As you examine each coin in a roll, check its condition with a magnifying glass. Do some look better than others? If so, why? What points in the coin's design tend to show wear?

For example, the search of five nickel rolls described in Chapter 3 turned up seven 1964 coins in varying conditions. Lining up some or all of the examples from worst to best is a good exercise in learning how to grade coins. Comparing them side by side illustrates how the Jefferson nickel looks as it begins to wear and which design areas tend to show the wear.

Shops and shows are also good places to look at lots of coins. Take your magnifying glass with you. If you see two coins of the same type and date but with different grades and prices, compare the two side by side and see what judgments you can make yourself about their condition.

Just like buying a used car, ultimately it comes down to whether a buyer likes the coin and is willing to pay the price.

MS-70

The grade mint-state-70 (MS-70) describes a flawless coin. The standard provides a theoretical top to the circulation-strike grading scale.

Grading world coins

Because of the wide scope of world coins, there is no comprehensive grading guide for the field. But the general descriptions for circulated coins given here can be applied to world coins, too. Traditionally, just the adjectives are used in grading world coins ("good," "fine," "extremely fine," and so on), not the accompanying numbers.

Why 1 to 70?

The 1-to-70 numerical grading scale is based on a system used by Dr. William H. Sheldon in his book "Early American Cents," first published in 1949. He used the scale to designate the condition of U.S. large cents, struck from 1793 through 1857 before they were replaced by the smaller one-cent coin used today.

1805 large cent.

"On this scale," Sheldon wrote, "1 means that the coin is identifiable and not mutilated—no more than that. A 70-coin is one in flawless Mint State, exactly as it left the dies, with perfect mint color and without a blemish or nick."

Sheldon's scale also had its pragmatic side. At the time, a No. 2 large cent was worth about twice a No. 1 coin. A No. 4 was worth about twice a No. 2, and so on up the scale.

Part 5

TAKING THE NEXT STEP

What to do when you're ready to move up from the basics

Chapter 24
The Coin Community

Coin collecting appeals to a wide range of people.

Coin collecting can accommodate any personality type. For those who like solitude, there can be peaceful evenings searching rolls of coins, admiring a completed collection or one in progress, or opening a book or magazine on the subject. For those who like camaraderie, there is an entire community out there that shares their interest and numerous venues for bringing them together.

Following is an overview of the coin community at large and resources for learning more about coins.

Organizations

National

The American Numismatic Association, founded in 1891 and federally chartered, is the nation's largest organization for coin collectors. Its headquarters in Colorado Springs, Colo., houses a first-class museum, the Edward C. Rochette Money Museum, which is open to the public.

Membership benefits include a subscription to *The Numismatist*, the association's official journal. Each monthly issue features articles on a wide range of numismatic topics along with reports on association news and events.

Members can also borrow books, auction catalogs, slide sets, and videos from the ANA's library, the Dwight N. Manley Library, which boasts more than 50,000 items. Members who borrow items pay for postage and insurance but no additional fee.

The ANA sponsors seminars on a wide range of numismatic topics at various locales throughout the country. Prominent among them is the association's Summer Seminar series, held annually in late June and early July at its headquarters in Colorado Springs. Attendance at the multi-day courses is designed to be affordable with a variety of lodging options and a meal plan.

The ANA also takes its seminar program on the road to the association's two annual conventions and to events sponsored by other numismatic organizations.

Regional

Regional coin organizations focus their activities on a certain part of the country, such as the Northeast or Midwest. Residency in the region, however, is usually not required for membership.

Prominent among these groups are the Central States Numismatic Society, Great Eastern Numismatic Association, New England Numismatic Association, and Pacific Northwest

The American Numismatic Association headquarters in Colorado Springs, Colo. Photo courtesy of ANA.

Numismatic Association. In addition, the Florida United Numismatists sponsors a large show and convention in January each year and boasts a large regional following in the Southeast.

See the Web site listings for contact information for most of these organizations.

State

Most states have clubs that focus on numismatic events and interests specific to the state. Again, residency in the state is usually not required for membership. See the Club Directory section of the ANA Web site (www.money.org) for information on state numismatic organizations.

Local

Many cities large and small have local coin clubs that meet regularly. The Club Directory section of the ANA Web site can help locate a club in or near a specific city. The events listings in local newspapers may help too.

Special interest

Some clubs focus on a specific collecting interest, such as commemoratives, silver dollars, or coins of a particular country. They draw their membership nationally and keep in touch through a quarterly or monthly journal. They also meet at larger numismatic events, such as the ANA conventions.

See the Club Directory section of the ANA Web site for listings and contact information.

Shows

Most numismatic organizations sponsor conventions and shows as part of their activities. They range from multi-day events with a national or even world focus, such as the ANA's annual conventions, to smaller one-day events sponsored by the local coin club.

The events usually include a bourse, an area where dealers set up to buy and sell coins. The local events may have a couple of dozen dealers; the larger events can have hundreds of dealers and booths for the U.S. Mint and other world mints. Both, however, give collectors the chance to look at a lot of coins in one location.

World mints participate in some larger shows, such as the ANA events.

The larger events also feature educational opportunities, such as competitive exhibits and seminars.

Numismatic periodicals, such as the monthly *Coins* magazine, available on many newsstands, and the weekly *Numismatic News,* list upcoming shows throughout the country. The Numismaster Web site (www.numismaster.com) and the ANA Web site also list upcoming events.

Books

The following books, all by Krause Publications, provide more information on coins and can also help new collectors take the next step in their collecting pursuits. They are available at most bookstores, online booksellers, or directly from the publisher at www.krausebooks.com.

"North American Coins and Prices"

The bulk of this book contains value listings for U.S., Canadian, and Mexican coins, but it also provides basic information on grading, how coins are made, assembling a collection, caring for coins, and market updates. New editions are published annually.

"Standard Catalog of World Coins"

This multi-volume series, published since 1972 and known worldwide, lists and values every coin produced in the world since 1701. The books are broken down by century, and each volume can be purchased individually. A three-DVD set going back to 1801 is also available.

"U.S. Coins & Currency"

Part of the Warman's Companion series, this book provides comprehensive coverage of U.S. coins and extensive coverage of U.S. paper money, including background information on each type of note. Introductory chapters cover some basic information about collecting U.S. coins and paper money.

"U.S. Coin Digest"

This hardcover book with a spiral binding provides comprehensive listings and values for all U.S. coins. Introductory material covers some of the basics of coin collecting. New editions are published annually.

"Warman's Coins & Paper Money"

Geared toward new collectors, this book is a value and identification guide for U.S., Canadian, and other world coins and paper money. The large-format book (8-1/2 x 11 inches) contains more than 3,000 photos.

"World Coins & Currency"

Part of the Warman's Companion series, this book provides a good overview of world coinage and paper money. It's a lower-cost alternative to the much bigger "Standard Catalog of World Coins."

Periodicals

The following publications provide news and information on a wide range of numismatic topics. In addition to their editorial content, their advertising provides a shop at-home marketplace for coins from dealers nationwide.

Coins

This monthly magazine (www.coinsmagazine.net) is available by subscription and on many newsstands. Its features and columns focus on U.S. coins. But it also covers the gamut of world numismatics. A U.S. coin value guide is included in each issue.

Coin Prices

Published six times annually, *Coin Prices* magazine (www. coinpricesmagazine.net) is a complete guide to U.S. coin values. It's available by subscription and on many newsstands.

Numismatic News

This weekly tabloid, founded in 1952, focuses on U.S. hobby news and events, but also includes features and columns covering a wide range of topics. A monthly value-guide supplement provides current listings for selected U.S. coins and market commentary and analysis. It's available by subscription and on some larger newsstands.

World Coin News

Similar in format to *Numismatic News*, the monthly *World Coin News* focuses on non-U.S. issues. It's available by subscription and on some larger newsstands.

Web sites

The following Web sites provide more information and resources on numismatic organizations, shows, publications, and coin collecting in general.

www.centralstates.info
Site for the Central States Numismatic Society. Provides news and information on this regional organization.

www.cmm.gob.mx
Site for the Casa de Moneda de México, Mexico's official mint.

www.coinpricesmagazine.net
Site for *Coin Prices* magazine. Includes subscription information and selected articles.

www.coinsmagazine.net
Site for *Coins* magazine. Includes subscription information, selected articles, and videos.

www.funtopics.com

Site for the Florida United Numismatists. Provides news and information on the organization.

www.krausebooks.com

Source for coin books published by Krause Publications.

www.mint.ca

Site for the Royal Canadian Mint, Canada's official mint. Includes ordering information for current issues.

www.nenacoin.com

Site for the New England Numismatic Association. Provides news and information on this regional organization.

www.numismaster.com

Sponsored by the publisher of *Numismatic News*, *Coins* magazine, and its related publications, the Numismaster site provides news and features, a collection management system, value guides, and more. A subscription is required to access some parts of the site.

2008 proof Bald Eagle silver dollar.

www.numismaticnews.net
Site for the weekly *Numismatic News*. Includes
subscription information, selected articles, and videos.

www.pnna.org
Site for the Pacific Northwest Numismatic Association.
Provides news and information on this regional
organization.

www.royalmint.com
Site for The Royal Mint of Great Britain, the country's
official mint. Includes ordering information for current
issues.

www.usmint.gov
Site for the U.S. Mint. Provides new-issue and historical
information. Collectors can also order current Mint
products, such as commemoratives, proof sets, and mint
sets.

www.worldcoinnews.net
Site for the monthly *World Coin News*. Includes
subscription information, selected articles, and videos.

Chapter 25
Moving Up

For some collectors, searching rolls of coins, watching their pocket change, buying new issues from the U.S. Mint, and buying inexpensive coins at shows or shops suit them just fine. They enjoy collecting at this level, are comfortable with it, and have no desire to move beyond it, nor should they feel any pressure to do so.

1916 Standing Liberty quarter.

For others, however, searching rolls of Lincoln cents merely whets their appetite for something bigger. For them, more than 200 years of U.S. coinage and centuries more of world coinage lie waiting. Gold coins, silver dollars, classic designs, and legendary world coinage can all provide a collecting experience rich in history and pride in ownership.

1921 Peace silver dollar.

Unlike plucking coins from circulation at face value, however, moving up to coins like the ones mentioned above may require an

1750 shilling of Great Britain.

outlay of hundreds or even thousands of dollars. That increases the chances for making mistakes, but the following tips for collecting more expensive coins will help limit those mistakes and lead to a rewarding collecting pastime.

Collect what you like

This remains coin-collecting rule No. 1 no matter the price. Collectors should always pursue a particular series or type set because something about it catches their interest. They shouldn't pursue it merely because others have said that's what they should collect or others have opined that it would be a good investment.

It may be the design. It may be the composition. It may be the subject depicted on the coin. It may be the country. It may be the era. Whatever the reason, the coins that capture an individual's interest are the coins he or she should collect.

Study

Once that coin series or type has captured your interest, learn as much as about it as you can. The word "study" is often associated with drudgery, but that is not the case if you have an intrinsic interest in the subject (remember: collect what you like).

It starts by learning the history of the country that issued the coin and the era in which it was issued. U.S. coins, for example, changed compositions at various times in the country's history in response to economic and political considerations. Learning a coin's historical context leads to a greater appreciation and understanding of the issue.

Next, learn about the coin itself. Specialized books and magazine articles focus on a particular series, such as Lincoln cents, Franklin half dollars, or Morgan silver dollars. This literature recounts the coin's history—how it came to be, who designed it, background on the design itself, and why it was discontinued if it is a design or denomination no longer produced.

These books and articles can also provide important information on individual dates within a series—which ones are common, which ones are scarce, subtle design changes from one year to the next, which dates usually have strong strikes, and which dates usually have weak strikes.

They may also provide information on grading the series, but a grading book, such as "The Official American Numismatic Association Grading Standards for United States Coins" or "Photograde," or both, should be a standard purchase for any coin collector, especially one pursuing more expensive coins. The book should be kept handy, referred to time and again, and eventually be worn out from use.

Finally, when you choose a type or series on which to focus, take advantage of every opportunity to look at a lot of examples of the coins at shows and shops. Take your magnifying glass with you. Compare coins of the same date; compare different coins of different dates. Compare condition and asking prices. Ultimately, you are the final judge as to whether you like the coin and are willing to pay the price.

1903-S Barber dime.

1908-O Barber half dollar.

Meet some dealers

Like shows, professional coin dealers can run the gamut from small-town, one-person operations to larger firms occupying multi-story buildings in metropolitan areas. Which one is right for you?

1913-D Buffalo nickel.

Choosing a coin dealer to work with in building your collection is like choosing any enterprise with which you do business. You walk into the business and you're just comfortable there. Maybe it's because you were greeted with a friendly hello and smile when you walked in. Maybe it's because you were allowed to browse and weren't pressured into a sale. Maybe it's because the business owner or an employee was knowledgeable and took the time to explain things and answer questions.

Or maybe it's because a friend or relative recommended the business. Whatever the reason, you end up going back and you develop a relationship with the business. When you walk through the front door, the business owner or employees know you and know your history as a customer.

The same is true with coin dealers. Some may not hit it off with you, but others might. Developing a business relationship with one or more dealers can be a great asset in building a collection. The dealer knows what you want and your price range, and can look for coins you want when the dealer is on a buying trip.

It's OK to bargain

It's OK to bargain with dealers at shows or shops, but be reasonable with your offers. It's OK to ask, "Is that your best price?"

It's not OK to berate a dealer if you think his or her prices are too high. Just move on to the next dealer at the show or move on to the next shop. The market ultimately will tell the dealer if his or her prices are too high.

1924 Buffalo nickel.

Oftentimes dealers will volunteer a small discount from the marked prices if you buy more than one coin. For example, if you select two coins and the total of the marked prices comes to $107, the dealer might take just $100.

Repeat business with the dealer might yield some discounts, too.

Auctions

Coin auctions are another fun and exciting way to build a collection. Some of numismatics' great rarities have made national headlines when they were sold at auction.

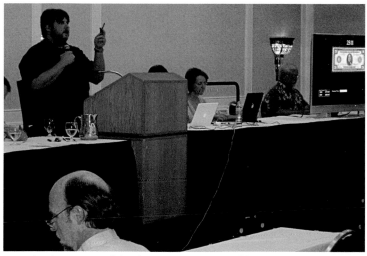

Auctions are a traditional and exciting way to add coins to a collection.

Major coins auctions are often staged as stand-alone events in ballrooms of large hotels. Many of the larger coin shows, including the annual ANA conventions, have auctions as part of the event's activities.

Auction companies usually require that you register as a bidder before the sale, but you don't have to be present to bid. Bids can also be submitted by phone and online.

Auctions are great educational opportunities even if you never bid at one. The major auction companies produce high-quality catalogs illustrating and describing each lot in the sale. The descriptions can be quite lengthy and filled with a wealth of historical and collecting information. The catalogs can be purchased in advance of the sale and are great additions to a numismatic library.

Watching an auction in person is also a great experience. By simply observing, a new collector can get a feel for how auctions work and their pace. And after the sale, the prices-realized list provides important market information.

1911-D gold $2.50.

If you do intend to bid at an auction, be sure to read carefully the sale terms as printed in the catalog. A thorough understanding of the auction company's obligations and your obligations as a bidder can prevent surprises and misunderstandings. For example, most auction companies charge a buyer's premium of 10-15 percent, so a collector must take this surcharge into consideration when determining how much to bid on a coin.

Coins as investments

Coins should not be purchased solely as investments unless you are playing the highest end of the market and buying some of the field's greatest rarities. That's not to say, however, that coins can't be good investments.

Some fabulous coin collections have been sold over the years and have reaped large sums for their owners or heirs. The biographies of those who assembled these great collections have one thing in common: These people were collectors first. They assembled these collections because they loved collecting coins. They studied the subject and were well schooled on what they were buying. They truly enjoyed their collections, and in time, they reaped financial rewards from them, too.

1873-CC (Carson City Mint) gold $10.

Be a collector first. Study what you're collecting. Know your coins. Make wise purchases. If you do, the financial aspects of coin collecting will take care of themselves.

Coins can increase in value over time; they can also decrease. But if you're a collector first, the market can never take away the enjoyment you get from the hobby.

Chapter 26
U.S. Coins on Review

U.S. coins provide a wealth of material for collectors. They offer a wide range of compositions, design styles, subjects, and sizes. The following pages provide a summary of all U.S. coins struck for circulation. Not included are commemoratives and American Eagle bullion coins. For a complete listing of U.S. coins, including individual date and mintmark combinations, and values in various grades, see the book "U.S. Coin Digest."

Value ranges listed are approximate retail prices (what you can expect to pay if you purchase the coin from a dealer) for more common dates in the series grading F-12 to XF-40. Key dates have higher values.

Diameters are in millimeters. Weights are in grams. Actual silver and gold weights are in troy ounces.

The various coin types are listed by their names commonly used in the hobby. The name usually refers to the main obverse design, but some coins are known by their designers' names.

Half cent

Liberty Cap, head facing left

Date: 1793. Designer: Henry Voigt. Diameter: 22. Weight: 6.74. Composition: 100 percent copper. **Value: $6,750-17,000.**

Liberty Cap, head facing right

Dates: 1794-1797. Designer: Robert Scot (1794) and John Smith Gardner (1795). Diameter: 23.5. Weight: 6.74 (1794-1795) and 5.44 (1795-1797). Composition: 100-percent copper. **Value: $750-6,000.**

Draped Bust

Dates: 1800, 1802-1808. Designer: Robert Scot. Diameter: 23.5. Weight: 5.44. Composition: 100-percent copper. **Value: $100-950.**

Classic Head

Dates: 1809-1811, 1825-1826, 1828-1829, 1831-1836. Designer: John Reich. Diameter: 23.5. Weight: 5.44. Composition: 100-percent copper. **Value: $70-250.**

Braided Hair

Dates: 1840-1857. Designer: Christian Gobrecht. Diameter: 23. Weight: 5.44. Composition: 100-percent copper. **Value: $90-3,000.**

Large cent

Flowing Hair, chain reverse

Date: 1793. Designer: Henry Voigt. Diameter: 26-27. Weight: 13.48. Composition: 100-percent copper. **Value: $15,000-33,000.**

Flowing Hair, wreath reverse

Date: 1793. Designer: Henry Voigt. Diameter: 26-28. Weight: 13.48. Composition: 100-percent copper. **Value: $4,000-12,000.**

Liberty Cap

Dates: 1793-1796. Designer: Joseph Wright (1793-1795) and John Smith Gardner (1795-1796). Diameter: 29. Weight: 13.48 (1793-1795) and 10.89 (1795-1796). Composition: 100-percent copper. **Value: $650-3,750.**

Draped Bust

Dates: 1796-1807. Designer: Robert Scot. Diameter: 29. Weight: 10.98. Composition: 100-percent copper. **Value: $150-400.**

Classic Head

Dates: 1808-1814. Designer: John Reich. Diameter: 29. Weight: 10.98. Composition: 100-percent copper. **Value: $200-2,500.**

Coronet

Dates: 1816-1839. Designer: John Reich. Diameter: 28-29. Weight: 10.89. Composition: 100-percent copper. **Value: $35-200.**

Braided Hair

Dates: 1840-1857. Designer: Christian Gobrecht. Diameter: 27.5. Weight: 10.89. Composition: 100-percent copper. **Value: $40-80.**

Small cent

Flying Eagle

Dates: 1856-1858. Designer: James B. Longacre. Diameter: 19. Weight: 4.67. Composition: 88-percent copper, 12-percent nickel. **Value: $40-300.**

Indian Head

Dates: 1859-1909. Designer: James B. Longacre. Diameter: 19. Weight: 4.67 (1859-1864) and 3.11 (1864-1909). Composition: 88-percent copper, 12-percent nickel (1859-1864) and 95-percent copper, five-percent tin and zinc (1864-1909). **Value: $3-200.**

Lincoln, wheat reverse

Dates: 1909-1958. Designer: Victor D. Brenner. Diameter: 19. Weight: 3.11 (1909-1942, 1944-1958) and 2.7 (1943). Composition: 95-percent copper, five-percent tin and zinc (1909-1942); zinc-coated steel (1943); and 95-percent copper, five-percent zinc (1944-1958). **Value: 30 cents-$50.**

Lincoln, Memorial reverse

Dates: 1959-present. Reverse designer: Frank Gasparro. Diameter: 19. Weight: 3.11 (1959-1982) and 2.5 (1982-present). Composition: 95-percent copper, five-percent tin and zinc (1959-1962); 95-percent copper, five-percent zinc (1962-1982); and 97.6-percent zinc, 2.4-percent copper (1982-present). **Value: Nominal except for some scarce varieties.**

Two-cent

Dates: 1864-1873. Designer: James B. Longacre. Diameter: 23. Weight: 6.22. Composition: 95-percent copper, five-percent tin and zinc. **Value: $20-130.**

Silver three-cent

Type 1 (no outlines in star)

Dates: 1851-1853. Designer: James B. Longacre. Diameter: 14. Weight: 0.8. Composition: 75-percent silver, 25-percent copper. Actual silver weight: 0.0193. **Value: $40-65.**

Type 2 (three outlines in star)

Dates: 1854-1858. Designer: James B. Longacre. Diameter: 14. Weight: 0.75. Composition: 90-percent silver, 10-percent copper. Actual silver weight: 0.0218. **Value: $45-130.**

Type 3 (two outlines in star)

Dates: 1859-1873. Designer: James B. Longacre. Diameter: 14. Weight: 0.75. Composition: 90-percent silver, 10-percent copper. Actual silver weight: 0.0218. **Value: $45-625.**

Nickel three-cent

Dates: 1865-1889. Designer: James B. Longacre. Diameter: 17.9. Weight: 1.94. Composition: 75-percent copper, 25-percent nickel. **Value: $20-450.**

Half dime

Flowing Hair

Dates: 1794-1795. Designer: Robert Scot. Diameter: 16.5. Weight: 1.35. Composition: 89.24-percent silver, 10.76-percent copper. Actual silver weight: 0.0388. **Value: $1,350-4,800.**

Draped Bust, small eagle

Dates: 1796-1797. Designer: Robert Scot. Diameter: 16.5. Weight: 1.35. Composition: 89.24-percent silver, 10.76-percent copper. Actual silver weight: 0.0388. **Value: $2,000-7,000.**

Draped Bust, heraldic eagle

Dates: 1800-1803, 1805. Designer: Robert Scot. Diameter: 16.5. Weight: 1.35. Composition: 89.24-percent silver, 10.76-percent copper. Actual silver weight: 0.0388. **Value: $1,500-5,500.**

Liberty Cap

Dates: 1829-1837. Designer: William Kneass. Diameter: 15.5. Weight: 1.35. Composition: 89.24-percent silver, 10.76-percent copper. Actual silver weight: 0.0388. **Value: $50-140.**

Seated Liberty

Dates: 1837-1873. Designer: Christian Gobrecht. Diameter: 15.5. Weight: 1.34 (1837-1853) and 1.24 (1853-1873). Composition: 90-percent silver, 10-percent copper. Actual silver weight: 0.388 ounces (1837-1853) and 0.0362 ounces (1853-1873). **Value: $60-500.**

Nickel five-cent

Shield

Dates: 1866-1883. Designer: James B. Longacre. Diameter: 20.5. Weight: 5. Composition: 75-percent copper, 25-percent nickel. **Value: $25-750.**

Liberty

Dates: 1883-1913. Designer: Charles E. Barber. Diameter: 21.2. Weight: 5. Composition: 75-percent copper, 25-percent nickel. **Value: $5-100.**

Buffalo

Dates: 1913-1921, 1923-1931, 1934-1938. Designer: James Earle Fraser. Diameter: 21.2. Weight: 5. Composition: 75-percent copper, 25-percent nickel. **Value: $3-300.**

Jefferson

Dates: 1938-present. Designer: Felix Schlag. Diameter: 21.2. Weight: 5. Composition: 75-percent copper, 25-percent nickel (1938-1942, 1946-present); 56-percent copper, 35-percent silver, nine-percent manganese (1942-1945). Actual silver weight: 0.0563 (1942-1945). **Value: 20 cents-$2 for pre-1959 dates.**

Dime

Draped Bust, small eagle

Dates: 1796-1797. Designer: Robert Scot. Diameter: 19. Weight: 2.7. Composition: 89.24-percent silver, 10.76-percent copper. Actual silver weight: 0.0775. **Value: $3,500-8,000.**

Draped Bust, heraldic eagle

Dates: 1798, 1800-1805, 1807. Designer: Robert Scot. Diameter: 19. Weight: 2.7. Composition: 89.24-percent silver, 10.76-percent copper. Actual silver weight: 0.0775. **Value: $800-4,500.**

Liberty Cap

Dates: 1809, 1811, 1814, 1820-1825, 1827-1837. Designer: John Reich. Diameter: 18.8 (1809-1828) and 18.5 (1828-1837). Weight: 2.7. Composition: 89.24-percent silver, 10.76-percent copper. Actual silver weight: 0.0775. **Value: $50-450.**

Seated Liberty

Dates: 1837-1891. Designer: Christian Gobrecht. Diameter: 17.9. Weight: 2.67. Composition: 90-percent silver, 10-percent copper. Actual silver weight: 0.0773. **Value: $10-1,000.**

Barber

Dates: 1892-1916. Designer: Charles E. Barber. Diameter: 17.9. Weight: 2.5. Composition: 90-percent silver, 10-percent copper. Actual silver weight: 0.0724. **Value: $3-500.**

Mercury

Dates: 1916-1921, 1923-1931, 1934-1945. Designer: Adolph A. Weinman. Diameter: 17.9. Weight: 2.5. Composition: 90-percent silver, 10-percent copper. Actual silver weight: 0.0724. **Value: $2-65.**

Roosevelt

Dates: 1946-present. Designer: John R. Sinnock. Diameter: 17.9. Weight: 2.5 (1946-1964) and 2.27 (1965-present). Composition: 90-percent silver, 10-percent copper (1946-1964) and clad layers of 75-percent copper and 25-percent nickel bonded to a pure-copper core (1965-present). Actual silver weight: 0.0724 (1946-1964). **Value: up to $3 for some pre-1965 dates.**

20-cent

Dates: 1875-1878. Designer: William Barber. Diameter: 22. Weight: 5. Composition: 90-percent silver, 10-percent copper. Actual silver weight: 0.1447. **Value: $120-400.**

Quarter

Draped Bust, small eagle

Date: 1796. Designer: Robert Scot. Diameter: 27.5. Weight: 6.74. Composition: 89.24-percent silver, 10.76-percent copper. Actual silver weight: 0.1935. **Value: $28,000-42,500.**

Draped Bust, heraldic eagle

Dates: 1804-1807. Designer: Robert Scot. Diameter: 27.5. Weight: 6.74. Composition: 89.24-percent silver, 10.76-percent copper. Actual silver weight: 0.1935. **Value: $500-2,850.**

Liberty Cap

Dates: 1815, 1818-1825, 1827-1828, 1831-1838. Designer: John Reich (1815-1828) and William Kneass (1831-1838). Diameter: 27 (1815-1828) and 24.3 (1831-1838). Weight: 6.74. Composition: 89.24-percent silver, 10.76-percent copper. Actual silver weight: 0.1935. **Value: $100-2,000.**

Seated Liberty

Dates: 1838-1891. Designer: Christian Gobrecht. Diameter: 24.3. Weight: 6.68. Composition: 90-percent silver, 10-percent copper. Actual silver weight: 0.1934. **Value: $30-1,200.**

Barber

Dates: 1892-1916. Designer: Charles E. Barber. Diameter: 24.3. Weight: 6.25. Composition: 90-percent silver, 10-percent copper. Actual silver weight: 0.1809. **Value: $20-450.**

Standing Liberty

Dates: 1916-1921, 1923-1930. Designer: Hermon A. MacNeil. Diameter: 24.3. Weight: 6.25. Composition: 90-percent silver, 10-percent copper. Actual silver weight: 0.1809. **Value: $5-725.**

Washington

Dates: 1932, 1934-1974, 1976-present. Designer: John Flanagan. Diameter: 24.3. Weight: 6.25 (1932-1964) and 5.67 (1965-present). Composition: 90-percent silver, 10-percent copper (1932-1964) and clad layers of 75-percent copper and 25-percent nickel bonded to a pure-copper core (1965-present). Actual silver weight: 0.1809 (1946-1964). **Value: $3-50 for pre-1965 dates.**

Half dollar

Flowing Hair

Dates: 1794-1795. Designer: Robert Scot. Diameter: 32.5. Weight: 13.48. Composition: 89.24-percent silver, 10.76-percent copper. Actual silver weight: 0.3869. **Value: $1,600-35,000.**

Draped Bust, small eagle

Dates: 1796-1797. Designer: Robert Scot. Diameter: 32.5. Weight: 13.48. Composition: 89.24-percent silver, 10.76-percent copper. Actual silver weight: 0.3869. **Value: $60,000-115,000.**

Draped Bust, heraldic eagle

Dates: 1801-1803, 1805-1807. Designer: Robert Scot.
Diameter: 32.5. Weight: 13.48. Composition: 89.24-percent
silver, 10.76-percent copper. Actual silver weight: 0.3869.
Value: $250-8,100.

Liberty Cap

Dates: 1807-1815, 1817-1836. Designer: John Reich.
Diameter: 32.5. Weight: 13.48. Composition: 89.24-percent
silver, 10.76-percent copper. Actual silver weight: 0.3869.
Value: $50-800.

Bust

Dates: 1836-1839. Designer: Christian Gobrecht. Diameter: 30. Weight: 13.36. Composition: 90-percent silver, 10-percent copper. Actual silver weight: 0.3867. **Value: $80-900.**

Seated Liberty

Dates: 1839-1891. Designer: Christian Gobrecht. Diameter: 30.6. Weight: 13.36 (1839-1853), 12.44 (1853-1873), and 12.5 (1873-1891). Composition: 90-percent silver, 10-percent copper. Actual silver weight: 0.3867 (1839-1853), 0.36 (1853-1873), and 0.3618 (1873-1891). **Value: $40-400.**

Barber

Dates: 1892-1915. Designer: Charles E. Barber. Diameter: 30.6. Weight: 12.5. Composition: 90-percent silver, 10-percent copper. Actual silver weight: 0.3618. **Value: $30-1,000.**

Walking Liberty

Dates: 1916-1921, 1923, 1927-1929, 1933-1947. Designer: Adolph A. Weinman. Diameter: 30.6. Weight: 12.5. Composition: 90-percent silver, 10-percent copper. Actual silver weight: 0 3618. **Value: $10-850.**

Franklin

Dates: 1948-1963. Designer: John R. Sinnock. Diameter: 30.6. Weight: 12.5. Composition: 90-percent silver, 10-percent copper. Actual silver weight: 0.3618. **Value: Up to $25 for some dates in grade XF-40.**

Kennedy

Dates: 1964-1974, 1976-present. Obverse designer: Gilroy Roberts. Reverse designer: Frank Gasparro. Diameter: 30.6. Weight: 12.5 (1964), 11.5 (1965-1970), and 11.34 (1971-present). Composition: 90-percent silver, 10-percent copper (1964); clad layers of 80-percent silver and 20-percent copper bonded to a core of 20.9-percent silver and 79.1-percent copper (1965-1970); and clad layers of 75-percent copper and 25-percent nickel bonded to a pure-copper core (1971-present). Actual silver weight: 0.3618 (1964) and 0.148 (1965-1970). **Value: Nominal for coins in circulated grades.**

Silver dollar

Flowing Hair

Dates: 1794-1795. Designer: Robert Scot. Diameter: 39-40. Weight: 26.96. Composition: 89.24-percent silver, 10.76-percent copper. Actual silver weight: 0.7737. **Value: $5,000-13,000.**

Draped Bust, small eagle

Dates: 1795-1798. Designer: Robert Scot. Diameter: 39-40. Weight: 26.96. Composition: 89.24-percent silver, 10.76-percent copper. Actual silver weight: 0.7737. **Value: $4,250-16,500.**

Draped Bust, heraldic eagle

Dates: 1798-1804. Designer: Robert Scot. Diameter: 39-40. Weight: 26.96. Composition: 89.24-percent silver, 10.76-percent copper. Actual silver weight: 0.7737. **Value: $1,200-4,300.**

Seated Liberty

Dates: 1839-1873. Designer: Christian Gobrecht. Diameter: 38.1. Weight: 26.73. Composition: 90-percent silver, 10-percent copper. Actual silver weight: 0.7736. **Value: $250-1,250.**

Morgan

Dates: 1878-1904, 1921. Designer: George T. Morgan. Diameter: 38.1. Weight: 26.73. Composition: 90-percent silver, 10-percent copper. Actual silver weight: 0.7736. **Value: $20-1,000.**

Peace

Dates: 1921-1928, 1934-1935. Designer: Anthony de Francisci. Diameter: 38.1. Weight: 26.73. Composition: 90-percent silver, 10-percent copper. Actual silver weight: 0.7736. **Value: $20-50.**

Clad dollar

Eisenhower

Dates: 1971-1974, 1976-1978. Designer: Frank Gasparro. Diameter: 38.1. Weight: 22.68. Composition: 75-percent copper and 25-percent nickel bonded to a pure copper core. **Value: Nominal in circulated grades.**

Anthony

Dates: 1979-1981, 1999. Designer: Frank Gasparro. Diameter: 26.5. Weight: 8.1. Composition: clad layers of 75-percent copper and 25-percent nickel bonded to a pure copper core. **Value: Nominal in circulated grades.**

Sacagawea

Dates: 2000-present. Obverse designer: Glenna Goodacre. Reverse designer: Thomas D. Rogers Sr. Diameter: 26.4. Weight: 8.07. Composition: 88.5-percent copper, six-percent zinc, 3.5-percent manganese, two-percent nickel. **Value: Nominal in circulated grades.**

Presidential

Dates: 2007-2016. Various designers. Diameter: 26.4. Weight: 8.07. Composition: 88.5-percent copper, six-percent zinc, 3.5-percent manganese, two-percent nickel. **Value: Nominal in circulated grades.**

2007: George Washington, John Adams, Thomas Jefferson, James Madison.

2008: James Monroe, John Quincy Adams, Andrew Jackson, Martin Van Buren.

2009: William Henry Harrison, John Tyler, James K. Polk, Zachary Taylor.

2010: Millard Fillmore, Franklin Pierce, James Buchanan, Abraham Lincoln.

2011: Andrew Johnson, Ulysses S. Grant, Rutherford B. Hayes, James A. Garfield.

2012: Chester A. Arthur, Grover Cleveland, Benjamin Harrison, Grover Cleveland.

2013: William McKinley, Theodore Roosevelt, William Howard Taft, Woodrow Wilson.

2014: Warren Harding, Calvin Coolidge, Herbert Hoover, Franklin D. Roosevelt.

2015: Harry S. Truman, Dwight D. Eisenhower, John F. Kennedy, Lyndon B. Johnson.

2016: Richard M. Nixon, Gerald Ford.

Gold dollar

Type 1

Dates: 1849-1854. Designer: James B. Longacre. Diameter: 13. Weight: 1.672. Composition: 90-percent gold, 10-percent copper. Actual gold weight: 0.0484. **Value: $100-1,500.**

Type 2

Dates: 1854-1856. Designer: James B. Longacre. Diameter: 15. Weight: 1.672. Composition: 90-percent gold, 10-percent copper. Actual gold weight: 0.0484. **Value: $200-1,500.**

Type 3

Dates: 1856-1889. Designer: James B. Longacre. Diameter: 15. Weight: 1.672. Composition: 90-percent gold, 10-percent copper. Actual gold weight: 0.0484. **Value: $150-600.**

Gold $2.50

Liberty Cap

Dates: 1796-1798, 1802, 1804-1807. Designer: Robert Scot. Diameter: 20. Weight: 4.37. Composition: 91.67-percent gold, 8.33-percent copper. Actual gold weight: 0.1289. **Value: $4,500-20,000.**

Turban Head

Dates: 1806, 1821, 1824-1827, 1829-1834. Designer: John Reich. Diameter: 20 (1808), 18.5 (1821-1827), and 18.2 (1829-1834). Weight: 4.37. Composition: 91.67-percent gold, 8.33-percent copper. Actual gold weight: 0.1289. **Value: $5,000-9,000.**

Classic Head

Date: 1834-1839. Designer: William Kneass. Diameter: 18.2. Weight: 4.18. Composition: 89.92-percent gold, 10.8-percent copper. Actual gold weight: 0.1209. **Value: $500-1,000.**

Coronet Head

Dates: 1840-1907. Designer: Christian Gobrecht. Diameter: 18. Weight: 4.18. Composition: 90-percent gold, 10-percent copper. Actual gold weight: 0.121. **Value: $150-2,500.**

Indian Head

Dates: 1908-1915, 1925-1929. Designer: Bela Lyon Pratt. Diameter: 18. Weight: 4.18. Composition: 90-percent gold, 10-percent copper. Actual gold weight: 0.121. **Value: $175-250.**

Gold $3

Dates: 1854-1889. Designer: James B. Longacre. Diameter: 20.5. Weight: 5.015. Composition: 90-percent gold, 10-percent copper. Actual gold weight: 0.1452. **Value: $800-2,500.**

Gold $5

Liberty Cap

Dates: 1795-1800, 1802-1807. Designer: Robert Scot. Diameter: 25. Weight: 8.75. Composition: 91.67-percent gold, 8.33-percent copper. Actual gold weight: 0.258. **Value: $3,000-7,000.**

Turban Head

Dates: 1807-1815, 1818-1834. Designer: John Reich. Diameter: 25. Weight: 8.75. Composition: 91.67-percent, 8.33-percent copper. Actual gold weight: 0.258. **Value: $2,500-5,000.**

Classic Head

Dates: 1834-1838. Designer: William Kneass. Diameter: 22.5. Weight: 8.36. Composition: 89.92-percent gold, 10.08-percent copper. Actual gold weight: 0.2418. **Value: $400-600.**

Coronet Head

Dates: 1839-1908. Designer: Christian Gobrecht. Diameter: 21.6. Weight: 8.359. Composition: 90-percent gold, 10-percent copper. Actual gold weight: 0.242. **Value: $200-5,000.**

Indian Head

Dates: 1908-1916, 1929. Designer: Bela Lyon Pratt. Diameter: 21.6. Weight: 8.359. Composition: 90-percent gold, 10-percent copper. Actual gold weight: 0.242. **Value: $300-500.**

Gold $10

Liberty Cap, small eagle

Dates: 1795-1797. Designer: Robert Scot. Diameter: 33. Weight: 17.5. Composition: 91.67-percent gold, 8.33-percent copper. Actual gold weight: 0.5159. **Value: $18,000-60,000.**

Liberty Cap, heraldic eagle

Dates: 1797-1804. Designer: Robert Scot. Diameter: 33. Weight: 17.5. Composition: 91.67-percent gold, 8.33-percent copper. Actual gold weight: 0.5159. **Value: $8,000-15,000.**

Coronet Head

Dates: 1838-1907. Designer: Christian Gobrecht. Diameter: 27. Weight: 16.718. Composition: 90-percent gold, 10-percent copper. Actual gold weight: 0.4839. **Value: $400-3,000.**

Indian Head

Dates: 1907-1916, 1920, 1926, 1930, 1932-1933. Designer: Augustus Saint-Gaudens. Diameter: 27. Weight: 16.718. Composition: 90-percent gold, 10-percent copper. Actual gold weight: 0.4839. **Value: $425-800.**

Gold $20

Liberty

Dates: 1849-1907. Designer: James B. Longacre.
Diameter: 34. Weight: 33.436. Composition: 90-percent gold,
10-percent copper. Actual gold weight: 0.9677. **Value: $800-2,500.**

Saint-Gaudens

Dates: 1907-1916, 1920-1933. Designer: Augustus Saint-
Gaudens. Diameter: 34. Weight: 33.436. Composition:
90-percent gold, 10-percent copper. Actual gold weight: 0.9677.
Value: $800-1,500.

More Coin Sense to Invest In

by Allen G. Berman

Whether you're a seasoned collector or a beginner with a piggy bank of potential the tips and tools for accurately identifying most coins and notes, contained in this full-color edition are second-to-none.

Softcover • 8-1/4 x 10-7/8 • 256 pages • 650 color photos
Item# Z2250 • $24.99

by Ken Potter and Brian Allen

Identify and easily determine the value of countless errors and varieties of coins with this one-of-a-kind guide, complete with 1,500+ large illustrations and grading scale.

Softcover • 6 x 9 • 320 pages • 1,500+ b&w photos
Item# Z3656 • $17.99

by David C. Harper, Editor; Harry Miller & Thomas Michael, Market Analysts

An active North American coins market demands the ready response of this new edition of the three-countries-in-one coverage of *North American Coins & Prices*. Research 45,000+ listings, pricing in 11 condition grades, and enjoy increased portability and search abilities with the **bonus DVD**.

Softcover • 6 x 9 • 624 pages • 3,000 b&w photos
Item# Z2406 • $22.99

Edited by Arlyn Sieber, Contributing Editor Mitchell A. Battino

The rush is on and gold is where it's at whether you're a collector or investor. Pick up tips about how and where to buy gold coins, how to use trend information to your advantage and much more.

Softcover • 6 x 9 • 272 pages • 400+ color photos
Item# Z1025 • $22.99

Order directly from the publisher at **www.krausebooks.com**

Krause Publications, Offer **NUB8**
P.O. Box 5009
Iola, WI 54945-5009
www.krausebooks.com

Call **800-258-0929** 8 a.m. - 5 p.m. to order direct from the publisher, or visit booksellers nationwide or antiques and hobby shops.

Please reference offer **NUB8** with all direct-to-publisher orders

Get News to Use at www.antiquetrader.com